S0-AKF-202

Love and Peace
By

[signature]

every
step
of the
way

foreword by Barbara Coloroso

Other Titles by the Authors

Eva Olsson

Unlocking the Doors: A Woman's Struggle Against Intolerance

Stronger Than Fire (Audio Compact Disk)

Remembering Forever: A Journey of Darkness and Light

Stronger Than Fire: The Eva Olsson Story (Digital Video Disk)

Jan Olsson

Keep It Simple, Make It Real:
Character Development in Grades 6-12

All rights reserved. No parts of this book may be reproduced or transmitted in any form or by any means electronic or mechanical, including photocopying, recording or any other information storage and retrieval system without the written permission of the publisher.

Copyright © 2011 by Eva Olsson

Printed in Canada by Rose Printing

ISBN 978-0-986-9150-0-0
Library of Congress Cataloging

10 9 8 7 6 5 4 3 2

Published by Eva Olsson
Bracebridge Ontario

*This book is dedicated to the millions of children
whose voices were silenced by hate.*

and in memory of husband and father

*Rude Olsson
(1926 – 1964)*

Life Lessons from
Every Step of the Way

In this book my mother shares her life stories and experiences, especially as they affected her parenting style and her determination to be a good role model. She saw passing on her legacy of caring, compassion and character to her son as the main reason for her survival. In relative terms, there are no comparisons between her life journey and the stories I share about my own life in this book. However, I've included my stories with the hope that some readers will learn from the hurdles I faced trying to reach my potential. My greatest challenges have come as a result of my struggles to accept my mother's life lessons, many of which can be found in this book, and are summarized on the following pages.

Jan Olsson

Never lose the passion for learning. It's never too late to confront one's fears and make the necessary changes in life.

Keep an open mind towards others and accept them for who they are. Be more patient and respectful of the process others must go through to work through their issues.

Parents have a responsibility to model the behaviour they expect to see in their children. The learning environment at home will largely determine a child's attitude toward others.

To feel good about oneself on the outside we have to accept who we are on the inside, and until we resolve our inner conflicts it will be difficult to move forward in a positive direction.

Have faith that the best possible solution will appear when it is most needed and have a positive outlook on life.

What we choose to do, and how we choose to do it, is a reflection of how comfortable we are with ourselves.

We are responsible for our own behaviour and the choices that we make – and we must consider the potential consequences before we take action.

Our attitude can lead us to success or failure. It begins by increasing our ability to separate perception from reality, and then focusing our energy on the decisions we have in front of us.

Sometimes our fears motivate us to push ourselves beyond our resources. We need to listen to our heart, mind and body so that we don't create suffering for ourselves.

We do not have the right to behave in an unkind manner towards someone who does something inappropriate to us.

It takes courage to look beyond the disappointments and painful experiences from our past and not let them control our future in order for us to reach our destiny.

Good relationships are built upon a foundation of deep friendship. When we are comfortable being with ourselves we are able to take the time necessary to cultivate a lasting connection with another person.

Children need to know the truth when they are ready to receive more information. When parents are willing to keep the lines of communication open with their children they provide an opportunity to discuss issues and concerns of importance.

Children respond best when they are given responsibility and treated with respect. Shielding children from reality will not help them develop a deeper understanding about situations that exist in life.

How our children will care for their children will depend on the degree of love and compassion that we give and demonstrate to them.

Table of Contents

Afterword
About the Authors

Acknowledgments

We gratefully acknowledge all those individuals who encouraged the writing of this manuscript. Thank you to Libby Charron, Don Smith, and Kari O'Neill who provided early feedback and positive suggestions for the completion of the story. Thank you to Ron Jacques for taking the time in his busy schedule to edit the book. Ron always looked for more, and because of his insights, we were fortunate to find it! Our good friend John Morrison was instrumental in helping us achieve clarity in our message. Thank you, John, for your caring and insights. Thank you to all of the other individuals who supported this project, especially Calvin O'Leary, Penny Arthur and Barbara Coloroso.

We would like to acknowledge the dedicated efforts of parents, teachers and school boards to nurture caring and compassionate adolescents.

Foreword

Looking in from the outside, Eva and her son, Jan, have a mother-son bond that is rich in its joys, heartaches, sorrows, and celebrations so common to the bonds that other mothers and sons cherish. As a widow, Eva raised Jan from his childhood through his teen years and into adulthood. The life lessons learned from his mom would guide Jan through his own marriage, fatherhood and his life-long career in education.

But the backdrop of this bond was far from common or even normal. Eva, and her sister, who she rescued from certain death, were the sole survivors of their large Jewish family all of whom died in the death camps during the genocide of World War II. Her own teen years were filled with horrors perpetrated by the Nazi "bullies." However, Eva was able to not only survive but also thrive in her adult years, marrying the love of her life and giving birth to her only son.

Eva refuses to surrender to the despair, bitterness, and contempt that could so easily consume her. Instead, she lives her own life with a passion and deep caring that gives her son the permission to share his own joys and heartaches, trials and troubles with her. She will not let her own story drown out his very real-life issues. She will not let her nightmares belittle his fears.

As you share their journey you may be jarred, as I was, by the contrast in Eva's heartbreaking story of profound loss and incomprehensible horror, and Jan's story of his own growing pains and tribulations typical of so many of us growing up in North America. However, underlying all of this is the wonderful human bond that Eva refused to abandon, refused to weigh against the inhumanity she endured, and instead, embraced fully with her own son. Teaching Jan the antidotes to the virulent hate that so easily rips apart the fabric of our humanity - caring deeply, sharing generously, helping willingly - she reaffirms her own love of life and allows Jan to celebrate his in his own way and in his own time - the true test of a mother's love, and of a son's unbreakable bond with his mother and their shared family history.

Barbara Coloroso
Author *Kids Are Worth It! Raising Responsible, Resilient and Compassionate Children* and *Extraordinary Evil: A Brief History of Genocide … and why it matters*

Introduction

My mother grew up in Hungary in a very strict Hasidic Jewish family. At the age of 19 she was taken away in a boxcar by the Nazis, along with the rest of her family, to the concentration camps in Auschwitz-Birkenau. Fortunately she survived, and while working in Sweden following the war, found love, security, and peace of mind after marrying her husband, Rude. They travelled across the Atlantic to Canada in 1951 to find a safer life, as many other young couples did. The Korean War was happening at the time and my mother was afraid there would be another war in Europe. Six months after they had arrived, my father came to like Canada and convinced my mother to settle here.

I was born on September 15, 1954 in Montreal. I would become my parents' only child – my twin sister died six hours before being delivered. My childhood was not easy. When I was ten years old my father died as a result of being hit by a drunk driver, and my self-confidence was shattered. My teenage years were a very difficult and challenging time. I was desperately trying to find my identity throughout high school, while my mother was also attempting to rebuild her life after experiencing yet another tragedy. She struggled with many issues, including several unsuccessful relationships, attempting to regain the loving bond she had established with my father. I was trying to become a successful athlete, and find my first girlfriend – hoping that achieving these goals might make me feel better about myself and fill the void left by my sister's and father's passings. Navigating my way through each day required more courage than what I thought seemed humanly possible for a tall, lanky and self-conscious sixteen-year-old boy. In spite of all of the obstacles my mother had encountered throughout her life, she was determined to make a total commitment to raising me as her son. Thankfully, my mother was there for me – every step of the way.

I had some confidence-building experiences in high school, like playing sports and participating in physical education classes. I met a young lady in Grade 9 while participating in a one-off co-ed physical education class and thought she was more than well suited to fill the role of "love of my life." She was short, cute and had long shiny black hair, and her athletic and shapely body was of keen interest to me. We had fun and quickly became friends during this wonderfully exciting time. I felt more certain of myself having her as my girlfriend.

My mother and I lived in a modest bungalow. Late one night my girlfriend and I were down in the recreation room having an argument. It was the kind of disagreement that teenagers might share afterwards with a close buddy, but certainly not with an adult, let alone their parents. However, on this particular night my girlfriend and I decided we needed to seek advice from someone who could give us some trusted answers to our problems. We chose to connect with a source of guidance and wisdom that we both felt more than comfortable with – my mother. My mother had been a second mother to many of my friends, and at one time even took in a friend who had gotten into an abusive situation with his father. Our home was like a safe haven for young adults – myself included. My mother was a great listener. She cared about our lives, and shared with us a much wiser perspective on our teenage problems than we were capable of providing for ourselves. The fact that my mother had lived a very sheltered childhood, and had survived the Holocaust, did not diminish her ability to relate to us as teenagers. She provided us with the support we needed, which was based on the moral code she had developed from her own life experiences. I trusted my mother and often had discussions with her about topics that I know my friends would never have with their parents.

My girlfriend, my mother and I ended up talking in the basement until the early hours of the morning. The recreation room was where we often went to have our long discussions. The image of the three of us sitting around the old Franklin wood-burning stove, working through my struggling relationship, remains etched in my mind. I've asked myself, "What teenage boy would want to ask his mother to mediate a quarrel with his girlfriend?" But what happened that night really was more about my relationship with my mother and the level of trust I had with her, and still do to this day! When I asked my mother how she felt about being awakened so late that night, she said it was important for her to be part of my life and it was better that I talk to her rather than strangers. She was sad that my dad, Rude, was not there for me to talk to, and felt it was her responsibility to ensure that she was there to support me at all times. The freedom my mother gave me to speak openly became one of the cornerstones of our relationship. I was deeply blessed to have her loving support.

Today, our lives don't seem to be getting any easier, but they are getting better. I owe my perseverance, passion for learning and discovery, and the development of my core values to my mother, Dr. Eva Olsson, Holocaust survivor, national bestselling author, public speaker, grandmother and friend.

I am now fifty-six years old. My mother is eighty-six. We both experience struggles and triumphs as we continue our complex journey together. Those of you who have read my mother's book *Unlocking the Doors: A Woman's Struggle Against Intolerance*, will know of her story of survival. My personal journey pales in comparison to the atrocities that she experienced during the Holocaust. However, over the last fifty-six years my mother and

I have developed an incredibly deep relationship that is filled with opportunities for learning and growth. My mother brings understanding and reason to my journey, which is even more incredible given that good portions of her journey lacked both.

My mother and I decided to write this book to share some of our life experiences and illustrate how they have provided us with opportunities for learning. Most particularly, we want to explore what she has taught me through our intimate and intense relationship as mother and son. Time is precious and for a number of years we have felt that our story needed to be told. I imagined that the magic of our story would inspire the next generation of youth to reflect upon their relationships and gain insights into their own experiences.

This book is specifically intended for use by middle- and secondary-school teachers and their students. Teachers can use these stories to prompt student reflection, discussion and writing on topics related to character development, history and literature. The engaging stories told by mother and son will also make this book of particular interest to anyone who has a rich and complex relationship with their parent or child.

The book is organized into fifteen chapters. Each chapter title is created using an appropriate quote that introduces a message to the reader, followed by short stories and brief reflections by my mother and me. Her voice is written in italics.

As a high-school principal I was passionate about nurturing a positive school climate based on respect, trust, honesty, empowerment and caring for our personal environment. My mother's mission since 1996 has been very similar, as she has tried to influence the moral development of youth by challenging them to become more accepting, compassionate and responsible citizens. Now my mother and I have been given the opportunity and time to work together on this project. Whether you are a teacher, parent or student trying to answer questions about your own journey, it is our hope that this book will inspire you to reflect on your own personal stories and find the path you desire.

A Short Story ...

Once a big fat Mouse and a lively little Mouse were hopping along together when they had the misfortune of jumping into a pail of fresh milk. They swam for hours and hours hoping to get out somehow, but the sides of the pail were steep and slippery and death seemed to be certain. When the big Mouse was exhausted he lost courage. There seemed no hope of rescue. "Why keep struggling against the inevitable? I cannot swim any longer," he moaned. "Keep on! Keep on!" urged the little Mouse, who was still circling the pail. So they went on for a while. But the big Mouse decided it was no use. "Little brother, we may as well give up," he gasped. "I am going to quit struggling." Now only the little Mouse was left. He thought to himself. "Well, to give up is to be dead, so I will keep swimming." Two more hours passed and the tiny legs of the determined little Mouse were almost paralyzed with exhaustion. It seemed as if he could not keep moving for another minute. But he thought of his dead friend, and intoxicated with determination, the little Mouse kept on swimming around and around the pail, chopping the milk into white waves. After a while, just as he felt completely numb and thought he was about to drown, he suddenly felt something solid under him. To his astonishment, he saw that he was resting on a lump of butter which he had churned by constant paddling! And so the successful little Mouse leaped out of the milk pail to freedom.

1

It's an endless search; sometimes the more
we search, the more we want to know.

On February 26, 1962, while driving to work, my husband was hit
head-on by a man driving under the influence of alcohol. It was a
shocking and horrifying experience to see my husband in that
smashed-up condition, with multiple injuries to the head, chest, and
knee. Three months later, with the help of eleven doctors, Rude was fi-
nally released from hospital in the third week of May. By late summer
of 1962 Rude had made a reasonable recovery and was well enough
to return to work – but by the fall of 1963 he was losing his sight and

could no longer drive. I was helping him into the car one day and he started to shake. That was the beginning of several convulsions resulting in him being hospitalized for another three months.

In the spring of 1964, each and every day I followed the doctor's suggestion and took Rude down to the Rehabilitation Centre near Sunnybrook Hospital in Toronto. Around 11 a.m. on June 2, the Rehab Centre called and asked me to come and take Rude home, as he wasn't doing as well as they would have liked. Actually Rude suffered a small stroke while he was there. It didn't paralyze him but he was too sick to take part in the program, so I picked him up at the centre and called the doctor, who ordered me to keep him in bed.

A few days later I looked out my kitchen window and saw a man in his pajamas walking with a cane. My God, it was my husband, Rude! He didn't know where he was. I ran out, helped him back into the house and called Dr. McGregor, our family doctor, who came over and made arrangements with the hospital in Richmond Hill to admit him. When I was visiting him one day he spoke to me in Swedish, "What are you doing here? Go home and look after the twins." Rude did not remember that our newborn twin daughter had died ten years earlier *in 1954, six hours before birth. He had lost all sense of time.*

A couple of months after that, the doctors talked about his condition and advised me to put him in Queen Elizabeth Hospital in Toronto. I knew I was never going to bring him home. He wasn't there more than two or three weeks when they called and told me they'd had to take Rude by ambulance to St. Joseph's Hospital, also in Toronto, as they didn't have the facilities to care for him at Queen Elizabeth. They put him in a ward at first and about a week later transferred him to a private room. He was deteriorating very rapidly. He had developed rales (the death rattle), so I knew the end was drawing near.

One day our son Jan asked to go to the hospital with me. When we got there Rude was unconscious, so Jan shook his dad's leg and touched his hands several times and said, "Dad, wake up – it's me, Jan." The pain on our son's face was unbearable and I turned away and walked to the window. This happened on Wednesday afternoon and on Thursday, September 24, at 7:00 in the evening, my darling husband Rude Olsson was dead.

When I look back on what happened, I appreciate the legacy that my husband left behind by showing me unconditional acceptance, love and compassion. I have held these values very dear to my heart; they are the values I speak of when I am in schools, and the values I have tried to convey to my son as he was growing up. Jan did not learn from me that using alcohol and drugs numbs pain, or that anger and the judgment of others provides one with relief from personal hardships. No matter how hard I tried as a single parent to reinforce positive values in my son, he was still a vulnerable teenager susceptible to the influences of his friends.

When my husband passed away I felt like my world had caved in on me. I was very unsure of myself, and wondered how I was going to raise a ten-year-old boy on my own, since I didn't have an education or the training to make a living for myself. I realized that I had some incredible challenges before me. I was very grateful to my son as he entered high school. He was a great support to me, which allowed me to continue one day at a time. I was blessed to have a good son and I took pride in him. It also became clear to me that I needed to be there for him at all times.

When I was a child my mother and I had a very strong bond

between us. However, there were times throughout my teenage years when I deliberately challenged her with the intention of establishing my independence. Thankfully, she didn't have knowledge of some of the more foolish and irresponsible decisions I made. One of the lowest points for me, and possibly for my mother, was when I came home one night from a friend's house. I hung out with a couple of guys in high school who had fathers who were heavy drinkers. At one of their homes there was always a liberal supply of alcohol around and we used to steal the odd bottle, and siphon off whatever we thought we could take without getting caught. Each year my friend's dad would buy a couple of cases of whiskey, so it was easy to sneak a bottle. We didn't know good whiskey from bad, but this stuff tasted awful, and I remember walking home one night by myself, having had too much to drink in too short a period of time. When I got home I snuck through the door and into my bedroom hoping I wouldn't get caught. Around 6:30 a.m. I woke up feeling really sick. By the time my mother came into my room to see what all the noise was about I was heading for the bathroom. It was the worst drinking experience I ever had and my mother made it very clear that she was extremely disappointed in me. I think I really frightened her because she realized how much trouble my friends and I were getting into. All I remember was the stale smell of whiskey and the sour taste of bile in my mouth.

That morning I promised my mother that I would never drink again – but that promise didn't last very long. A short time later I purchased a six-pack of beer, which I stashed away in a small wooden night table my father had made in his basement shop. One day while my mother was dusting in my room she opened the cabinet door where the beers were hidden. As soon as I saw her looking inside I completely lost control and started yelling at her at the top of my lungs. She turned towards me with a look of confusion and shock on her face. I realized that she didn't know why I was yelling at her, because she hadn't noticed the beer in the cabinet. I quickly changed my tone and began backtracking by offering an apology, using my lack of sleep as an excuse for my erratic behaviour. This was not the last time I would lash out towards my mother with harsh words that were unjustified. Interestingly, it was shortly after this incident that I came to my own realization about the harm that the drinking was doing, and it became much less of an issue during my last two years of high school. I could see that my friends were not very concerned about the direction I was going. Every one of us was into partying; however, I was starting to get into trouble with my mother because I was hosting the parties and the house was starting to get damaged. Throughout these years my mother never abandoned me. Regardless of how idiotic my actions were she was there to guide me through the next step of my journey.

Young teenagers often hide what they do from their parents because they have an unrealistic sense of confidence and act like they are invincible. What they don't understand is that by drinking so much they are harming themselves physically by damaging their internal organs. I worried about what my son was doing to his body and his health. When I became aware of the fact that my son had alcohol-related issues I knew that I couldn't condone his behaviour. I couldn't afford to lose him because he was the only remaining family I had. The rest of my family had either died in the camps or had abandoned me; I was not going to abandon my own son. I called his drinking buddies' parents – all of them. After those calls only one of those boys remained Jan's friend – and I was okay with that.

My mother and I tend to do a lot of philosophizing on various topics and every decision that is up for debate creates a potential conflict between us. She must have been incredibly frustrated over the years as I continually tried to prove her wrong with my closed-minded views. My mother had been denied an education, and as a single immigrant parent she had very little knowledge of the North American way of life. At times it was very difficult for her to enforce a harsh approach to discipline while raising me. After losing her husband, she didn't want to lose her son as well, so she would tell herself, "I'm not going to rock the boat by reprimanding my son." I remember her trying to tell me that one of my friends was not the right person for me and I responded, "You're not going to tell me who I should choose as a friend." Despite my stubbornness, my mother continued to talk through issues with me and share her insights and moral lessons on life. She persevered through my teenage years; however, the conflicts between the two of us worsened as I finished my university education, found a job, got married, and became the father of three children.

For over fifteen years my mother provided daycare for my three children while she worked seven nights a week at a local hotel to make ends meet financially. She was a devoted Bubba, committed to teaching her grandchildren right from wrong, while providing a loving environment for them during the days that my wife and I were working. Throughout those years my mother and I managed to maintain a reasonably healthy adult-to-adult relationship; however, the disagreements that arose from our differing views on many issues, such as childrearing, continued to escalate. I became more confident about what my wife and I knew, and convinced that my mother's views were out of date and out of touch.

My mother and I never yelled at each other, nor did we use disrespectful language or call each other names. Our comments tended to be more philosophical in nature and sharply directed at the personal level. During a recent conversation, my mother reminded me of a particularly hurtful day about nineteen years ago when I arrived at her house at the end of the work day to pick up my children. It was common for us to take a few minutes to connect around the events of the day; I would get an update on the health and well-being of the kids, and my mother would discuss their behaviours. I would then proceed to tell her how their disciplining should be handled. I told my mother, "We (my wife and I) know what we are doing; we are educated." Not surprisingly, my comment really upset her. Over the years I had always used my mother's lack of education as a defense against her if I didn't agree with her point of view. I then tried to explain to her that I knew her really well because she was my mother and this upset her even more. She responded by saying, "Yes, but how much do you know the person that's on the inside of the mother?" I said, "I don't know," to which she responded, "Thank God I'm not educated – I might have turned out like you."

In recent years I have developed a deeper understanding for what it means to be an intelligent person. Those individuals who learn from their own life experiences, like my mother, are among the smartest people I have met. I have learned there is no substitute for this kind of learning, and I respect and admire my mother's intellectual abilities, despite the fact that she was denied a formal education. I was extremely fortunate that my mother was willing to spend thousands of hours raising my children. It afforded me the opportunity to pursue my career and personal interests without the added expense of child care. What I failed to recognize at the time was how valuable this experience was for my children.

My mother's home life as a teenager in Hungary, over seventy years ago, was the source of much of her pain. She was denied an education by someone who also thought he knew better than her.

Once every year a man came to the door to ask if there were any school-age children in the home. Our mother told us to hide in the wardrobe or under the bed before she opened the door. There were no toys lying around because we didn't have any in our home. I can still hear my mother saying, "No, there are no school-aged children here." Following their Hasidic beliefs, my parents did not send their children to public schools. My two brothers attended hider *(a Jewish school) only, for religious purposes. The tutors who schooled Hasidic girls had a very limited amount of schooling themselves. We learned all about the very limited Hasidic world but were denied contact with others and knowledge of the world outside. We were taught from childhood that females existed for bearing babies and doing household chores. We were first tutored in Yiddish from age six to nine or ten. We spoke only Yiddish in our home, as speaking Hungarian was considered* goyish *(gentile). Outside the home we had a choice of speaking Hungarian or Romanian. Although we were taught that if we lied our "tongues would be cut out," we saw our parents lie when it suited their fundamentalist needs.*

When I was around ten years of age I was sent to summer school where I was taught some Hungarian and more Yiddish. The school was a large converted home that had been donated by the Jewish community for the purpose of teaching underprivileged children in the summer. At this beautiful summer school I felt deprived and cheated because I wanted a full public education, not a narrow, self-interested and restricted education. I became resentful to the point that I was not

interested in learning what they were teaching. The more school I at-
tended, the more I resented my parents' way of living and their beliefs.
In spite of all this, I had respect for my parents while I was still living
under their roof. A turning point came when I was sixteen because I
had to choose between following my parents' wishes or developing my
own identity. I chose at that time not to have confrontations with them
because I respected their right to have their beliefs and I realized they
were not going to bend.

When I was 12 years old my mother explained to me why she didn't have a formal education. I always thought she was denied an education because of World War II. At that point, I didn't know that her parents were the reason she hadn't gone to school. I remember saying to her, "Mom, it's too bad you weren't educated. You would have made a good lawyer."

Having no formal education became a huge limitation for my mother, both financially and emotionally. While my father was in the hospital and his health continued to decline, my mother was approached by one of the nurses regarding a part-time job opportunity. The job involved working two half-days looking after two young boys in the nurse's home. The nurse's husband was a doctor and they needed the extra support. My mother was offered two dollars an hour, which was more money than she had ever made in Canada. She was overwhelmed with joy at the thought of working for such generous pay even though she had no formal education. One day the nurse offered my mother another job opportunity, saying, "I'm going to show you how to fill out the health card forms for our patients." My mother was petrified. She didn't want to tell the nurse that she didn't know how to write, so she quit the job for fear of being seen as incapable.

It wasn't until after my father's death that my mother's attitude toward her lack of education began to change. She used to go to the bank weekly to pay bills. Each time she approached the teller she would fumble in her purse and pretend that she had forgotten her glasses so that she wouldn't have to fill out a cheque or deposit slip. It bothered my mother so much that she went into the bank and lied to the teller. Finally, one day she asked herself, "How long am I going to pretend to forget my glasses? And why am I so afraid to fail?" At that moment she began to search deep inside herself and learned to accept the good person that she knew she really was. The next time she visited the bank she decided to go to the teller, explain that she couldn't write, and ask for help. When she did, the teller responded, "I'm happy to do that, Mrs. Olsson!" What resulted from these first courageous steps eventually became three thousand speaking engagements, a national bestselling autobiography and thousands of letters from individuals sharing their own stories of struggle and triumph. And she takes the time to read them all.

My mother tells students that she is envious of them, because they have been given an opportunity that she never had – the opportunity to learn. Being denied an education at a very early age left her with feelings of insecurity and inadequacy. When she was young she used to get spanked because of her open and defiant search for knowledge. It was not until she decided to take a really good look at herself that she began to unlock the doors created by her deprivation.

Now that I have raised three children of my own, I understand some of the challenges that my mother experienced trying to raise me. My grandmother used to say, "You don't have to be qualified to kill a chicken to know how to make a good pot of soup." My mother did an amazing job as a single parent raising me. She provided me with the opportunities she was denied, by giving me the encouragement, support and freedom to pursue knowledge, experience life for myself and express my feelings openly. But most importantly, I'm grateful to this day that my mother never gave up searching for the best way to raise me as her only child.

I learned from my mother to keep searching for the answers and never lose the passion for learning. I appreciate the legacy of unconditional acceptance, love and compassion that she has now passed on to me from my father, allowing me to continue my search for new knowledge and more meaning in life. It's never too late to confront one's fears and make the necessary changes in life.

It's an endless search; sometimes the more we search, the more we want to know.

2

When we lock others out, we lock ourselves in.

While my sister Fradel and I were both living in Sweden she got married and I was not invited to her wedding. Only the two of us from our family survived the camps, and she had now locked me out! At that point I wasn't married or engaged to a Swede; however, she didn't like the fact that I was working on the Sabbath that, according to the high orthodox beliefs, was forbidden. That is why she locked me out; needless to say I was devastated.

With the exception of a brief visit in Sweden in 1946 after our liberation from Bergen-Belsen concentration camp, I did not see my sister again until 1982 in Boston. That spring my son asked me to get in touch with my sister. I tried to explain to him what the Hasidim are like and that she would not want anything to do with me, but he felt that she might have changed since the war. Many years ago I had received a letter from my brother-in-law, David, who had been told by my friend Edith that Rude and I had left for Canada; she had given him our address in Montreal. He wrote me and his return address was on the envelope but for all those years I had kept the envelope but had not written back. When I finally agreed to write my brother-in-law and sister I received a quick response back telling me that she and her husband would be in Boston in April, as their youngest son, Haim, would be studying physics at Harvard. I had been given my nephew's phone number in Boston, so I called to make arrangements to meet them in the first week of May 1982.

On May 2, 1982 I arrived in Boston. I finally saw my sister again after 36 years, along with her husband, son and daughter-in-law. Fradel had ten children, but the son who was present was the only one who knew he had an aunt who had survived the Holocaust with their mother. All her children are Hasidic except this youngest son, Haim. Strangely, her husband, David, is not Hasidic either. The other sons spent most of their days in the synagogue while their wives were working. She showed me pictures of the other nine children, but all she talked about was their religious lives. Fradel expressed her pride in them and wished our parents could share her joy.

During dinner I told my sister that in Toronto I had talked to a rabbi from Szatmar, our hometown in Hungary. This rabbi was very liberal and had a large multi-racial and multi-religious congregation. He was open to and tolerant of other religions and said he would perform the Jewish marriage ritual for me if I wanted to get married. He felt that marriage should include rather than exclude people. I was excited to share this information with Fradel, hoping it might bring us closer together, but she started laughing and said to her husband, "Husband, did you hear this? Is this a rabbi? He is no rabbi." There was silence at the table. Clearly only Orthodox beliefs and believers were of any value to her.

We were supposed to walk around the university after dinner, but it started to rain, so my nephew and I went to the coffeehouse and had a three-hour conversation. His main concern was that I not hurt his mother. How could I do this? She had already hurt herself by ignoring God's Golden Rule: Love one another as we love ourselves. I couldn't condone her behaviour or forgive her for denying my existence to her family. I wondered if she had performed shiva, the ritual of sitting on the floor for seven days mourning the dead. She would have had to sit alone since nine of her children didn't know I existed. I have asked God to forgive her; it's between God and her. I knew that in order to free myself of anger I had to forgive her.

My nephew asked me what I would tell God when he called me home and I told him I would tell my God that I did the job he sent me down to do. He also wanted to know if his grandfather was a saint. I told him that my father was a human being with strengths and weaknesses. These two subjects were his only concern; there was no talk about his family, his studies or his life. As we parted at closing time he told me that he could understand my choice of a liberal lifestyle if it was the result of the horrors of the Holocaust. I told him I had been looking for a more open and tolerant way of life long before the war started. When we met again the next morning my sister announced in front of *everyone that she could not accept me as part of her family: "I cannot be any different than our father would have been." I was devastated to hear her cruel words and to be humiliated in front of my family. It was so unnecessary for me to travel from Toronto to Boston to suffer such cruel treatment. She knew what my lifestyle was before I went there, so I have to wonder what her real motives were in asking me to come to Boston. I didn't understand why she would want to cause me more pain by denying my existence, just because I didn't follow her religious beliefs. Why do people continue to cause so much pain for each other because of cultural, racial, religious, or national differences? I was very sad but I realized that Fradel had to live her life according to her beliefs and she could not accept me because I was so alien to her. Fradel lives the way my parents lived, not giving an inch or bending, and this reflects her interpretation of the messages she received at home. I also knew that I had to live my life as I saw fit. The life I am living reflects my lifelong desire for a more flexible or understanding way of life. I got up from the table and left for good.*

The hatred that the Nazi supporters directed towards the Jews can never be fully understood. But why would a woman who had experienced and survived the Holocaust choose to treat her only surviving family member, her sister, with the same kind of hatred and bigotry that she had experienced in the concentration camps herself? My mother taught me that no one deserves to be locked out. Regardless of gender, religion, colour, culture or sexual orientation, everyone should be acknowledged and appreciated; it's our attitude that makes us different.

In an attempt to protect and assert themselves, teenagers can be very hard on their peers; many choose to lock out their friends for minor reasons. My youngest daughter is enrolled in second-year nursing at university. I am amazed by her quiet, kind and conscientious manner. She invests a lot of time connecting with others via cell phone and chooses her social network very carefully. Within that social network she is quite loyal to those select individuals she calls friends. I remember a very difficult time for her when she had a falling out with one of her closest friends, Brittany. They had arranged one day to socialize after supper, and as the dinner hour passed, there was no phone call, no email, no text message – Brittany simply didn't show. My daughter didn't hear from her until several weeks later and the text message she received made no mention of any problem or mistaken booking on the night of the no-show several weeks earlier. In fact, the text message made no mention of the evening at all. My daughter was both angry and hurt. She had been shut out. Given the instant nature of today's electronic communication there was no excuse for Brittany not showing, or at least making the effort to contact my daughter to say why she could not make the commitment.

I am cautious about the potentially isolating nature of communicating via email or text messaging, and the lack of face-to-face contact. Technology has allowed us to distance ourselves from our own messages, while providing us with a false sense of privacy when communicating with others. My daughter and her friends spend a great deal of time trying to establish themselves as individuals within their social structure. As many girls (and boys) find, adolescence is littered with moments of isolation and loneliness. Does my daughter shy away from face-to-face conversations? My daughter had been locked out by her friend – but was that a good enough reason for her to do the same thing to her friend? Should she too ignore The Golden Rule? I really encouraged her to address the incident head-on, in a respectful and adult way. I suggested she contact her friend and let her know exactly how she felt about the night she was stood up, but she couldn't bring herself to do it – the risk of being shut out permanently was too great. Eventually, her silence "twigged" Brittany and an apology was received via email. Thankfully, that message began a conversation that allowed my daughter to express her unhappiness and disappointment.

There are many reasons why individuals may choose to lock others out. My mother was locked out because of her sister's religious prejudices. Perhaps Fradel was protecting herself from having to look at her sister's different views on life. We cannot be certain about her – or any individual's – need to hide and where the prejudice or fear may come from. The underlying attitudes are often learned from our parents and the environment in which we are raised. My mother would say that there is never a good enough reason to lock others out.

After my mother finishes her speaking presentation she finds that both students and educators often come forward to share their personal stories of being locked out. One educator told my mother that after his divorce his daughter didn't speak to him for ten years; another divorced person said it was four.

One of my mother's favourite sayings is, "If someone slaps you in the face, you don't turn your cheek to get slapped on the other side." It was a familiar lesson growing up, and one I tried to impress upon my own children. I've always felt very strongly that if someone does something hurtful to another person then they have a responsibility to fix it, by apologizing and changing their behaviour. If someone does something hurtful towards me, I have a great deal of difficulty trying to pretend that things are right between us until that person comes forward and clears the air. I make a point of getting back to someone when I feel that I may have offended them in some way.

I have found that people are reluctant to have honest conversations for fear of hurting someone or being hurt themselves. Fradel chose to ignore the issues with her sister and maintained a wall of silence for 65 years. When people don't come back I ask myself these questions: "What can I do about it now? Is this where forgiveness potentially heals the relationship? Do I keep giving after I have forgiven, or do I just forgive and wait for a potential response in the future?" My mother and I talk about her sister all the time. I keep asking her the same question over and over, "What will you do if Fradel continues to lock you out? After all, she is your only surviving family member."

Had my sister come to me with a sincere apology after ten or fifteen years of locking me out, it would have made a huge difference. If she had said to me, "I want you to be part of my family," it would have told me that even though she didn't like my choices, she was willing to accept me for who I am. That didn't happen, and now it's sixty-four years later and it still hasn't happened. You can go on for a lifetime waiting for small miracles to happen; I have experienced them. However, I don't believe a miracle will come from Fradel in Tel Aviv.

I learned from my mother to keep an open mind towards others and accept them for who they are. My mother continues to teach me this lesson – she knows that my communication with others doesn't always work out the way I think it should. I find that the more individuals try to protect themselves the less accepting they are of others. And I've learned to be more patient and respectful of the process others must go through to work through their issues.

3

We all have skeletons in our closet.

In the early 1940s my father came home and told us shocking stories that he had heard at the synagogue or read in the Jewish newspapers. A Polish man who had escaped from Poland came to my father's synagogue and told him that when the Germans arrived in Poland in 1939 they went to a Jewish home, took the male head of the household out and made him dig a big grave. He was forced to bury his family of nine alive and pour lye on them. Then they shot him and threw him in the grave. Soldiers who saw pregnant women on the street stabbed them in the stomach with their bayonets.

I can't imagine what it must have been like for a young child to hear these stories being told. Living with these memories must be painful, and certainly beyond the understanding of most. My mother says, "Every German was not a Nazi and every Nazi was not a German." Though she has forgiven those responsible for what they did to her, she believes that, morally and historically, she does not have the right to forgive those responsible for the deaths of six million Jews and five million others. Her pain is uncovered every time she speaks about what happened – it's like a skeleton hanging in her closet that jumps out of the darkness whenever she lets a little bit of light in.

In 1956 my mother and father moved to a small bedroom community north of Toronto with a population of nine thousand. Many of the homes were newer, small bungalows, built for young families. Typically, the mothers stayed home while the fathers travelled each day into Toronto to work. Every morning some young mothers in our neighbourhood would meet for coffee. They would move from one house to another, discussing their husbands' personal business and the lives of other people in the neighborhood. My mother was considered to be a new Canadian, and as a result, was never invited to be part of the "coffee-clique." She had hoped to escape this prejudice in a great country like Canada, but was shocked to find such blatant discrimination on the street that she now called home.

I attended a small elementary school a few blocks away from our home. It was close enough that I could walk to and from school each day. One day I arrived home after school with my new winter jacket muddied inside and out. My grandmother from Sweden had sent me the ski jacket as a gift. The gabardine coat had a lambskin lining and an unusual zipper on the side. It didn't look like a typical North American ski coat, and I was very proud to wear it.

It wasn't the first time I had come home with a muddy jacket. My mother asked me, "Who pushed you down?" I told her it was one of the boys who lived in our neighborhood. She decided to call my grade two teacher to see if she could get to the bottom of what was happening. I was an only child, and my mother always wanted to be sure that I was upholding the values she had taught me, and practicing them outside the home. When my mother spoke with her, the teacher said, "He's always the first to put his hand up with a question. He always wants to know more." My mother had instilled in me the importance of asking questions and always looking for more information.

The bullying continued so I decided to go to the principal of the school. When I shared with him what was happening in the schoolyard he responded by saying, "You know how kids are, kids will be kids." His attitude really disappointed me. In response I said to him, "These kids will replace you some day." A day after my meeting with the principal I received an unusual phone call from one of the parents in my neighborhood who happened to be the bully's mother. She told me I was cheeky and I wasn't sure what that meant. I explained to her that my reason for going to the principal was to make sure that my son had not provoked her son. She just hung up and never talked to me again.

By the time I was forty I had become a widow. Rude had died from complications resulting from his car accident. Some of the mothers on my street had completely cut me off when they realized that I had hidden the fact that I was a Jew and had survived the Holocaust. One teenager from our neighbourhood was walking past my house on the way home from high school and called out to me "You Jew." I lifted my head and said, "What's the problem? Are you jealous because you don't have the brain of Einstein?" I was shocked because I had never told any of the neighbours that I was Jewish. I was afraid to tell anyone for fear they wouldn't like me. It was a fear I had brought with me across the ocean, a fear that there were still bullies out there that would want to hurt me – and I was right. From that point on, I realized they knew I was Jewish.

One day my neighbour's son, who was also in high school, walked past our driveway, looked right at me, and made a spitting motion at the ground. I felt very sad that being European and Jewish meant that I would be looked down upon and considered less worthy of being treated with the respect and dignity that a human being would deserve. Soon after these incidents, a gentleman who lived on our street came over to the house with some pound cake. He was sorry to hear that Rude had passed away. When he gave me the cake he looked at me and said, "I don't know how you can live in this neighbourhood."

My telephone bill arrived in the mail each month at its usual time.

I would always open up the envelope and, as was customary for me to do, I examined all the numbers to make sure the bill was accurate. One particular month I noticed that some numbers were unfamiliar to me. I contacted the customer service department of the telephone company to investigate the discrepancy. None of my friends had that phone number so I asked, "Where is this number from? To whom does it belong?" The representative verified that the calls were made from my home number to a place where horses are boarded. I knew that one of our neighbours was involved with horses, so perhaps they had made the call. It was also clear that the call wasn't made from my house. In those days, when you made a collect call that was long distance, the operator would ask, "What's your number please?" – and you would give your number. What must have happened is the person who made the call used my phone number to charge it collect. I decided to confront my neighbour who I knew had an interest in a horse operation in another town. When I approached him he explained that he had given my home number because he did not want his wife to find out. The reason he didn't want her to know was because he had a mistress who worked at the horse stables.

We all have skeletons in our closet.

Shortly after I had learned about this escapade the neighbour's wife approached me. It turned out that she was also having an affair. She came over one evening to ask if I would give her kids supper from their leftovers. She explained to me how she felt about a man she worked with, and that her husband was working shift work that night so she was heading downtown to meet her lover.

It's interesting how well I could keep a secret. They both confided in me but I didn't feel I could disclose the other's affairs. While those things were going on in that household, it was their son who was making those racist gestures towards me. I often wonder if he would have behaved differently if his parents had modeled integrity.

I can empathize with my mother. Like her, I had never discussed my heritage with anyone. As a principal, I always had some fear in the back of my mind that I was in danger while working at my school. A number of the students had behaved very aggressively towards me and other staff. I would ask myself, "What's going on in their lives that makes them want to treat others with such rudeness and disrespect?" One time I was told by a student, "Fuck you, I hope you burn in an oven." I was shocked. In another situation, a male student created a poster, which he posted around the school that showed me holding hands with another person. The caption underneath read, "Stuck on Jew."

Children are not born racist. Each of us experiences circumstances that help us form our opinions about the world and the people who live in it. What the young German soldiers did to the Polish Jews in 1939 demonstrates that children can learn to interpret what it means to be different, depending on what they are taught by the adults around them. What did our neighbour's son hear from his parents that caused him to spit at my mother? The answer may never be known, but perhaps examining the learning environment of that boy a little more closely would provide some insights.

I believe in the influence of genetic factors. I have always wanted to know more about myself and where my personality characteristics came from. I'm sure a lot of it comes from my parents. Even today I do some things the same way my mama did. I have my father's skin colouring and curly hair from Grandfather Jankev. My father's father also had a philosophical side, as I do. My father's first cousins were modern, well-mannered ladies; I never saw them with a prayer book in their hands. Most of the members of my father's family were modern Jews so he infrequently spoke of them. He wanted no modern influences in the lives of his children. My parents were worried that we might adopt these outside influences as our own.

My mother taught me that making poor choices is a part of learning and growing. We first need to focus on correcting mistakes we have made ourselves, before judging the behaviours of others. The truth is we all have skeletons in our closet so we must focus on being true to who we are.

I learned from my mother that parents have a responsibility to model the behaviour they expect to see in their children. The learning environment at home will largely determine a child's attitude toward others, and what they will bring with them to school.

4

What is hidden within will dictate
what appears on the outside.

*As I entered my teens my father was very concerned about me. I had
my own ideas as to how far one should take religion and I feel my parents went overboard. Hasidic females had to wear long, thick, black
stockings, and dresses with long sleeves and long necks. They couldn't
look out the window because a boy might see them. Marriages were
arranged through a matchmaker, and they met the boy for the first
time when their parents met his. They got to see him for a half an hour
and that marriage was expected to last for the rest of their lives. I still
feel it's like throwing a piece of meat to the wolves, because there is no*

love. In spite of all this, I had respect for my parents while I was still living under their roof. A turning point in my life came when I was sixteen because I had to choose between following my parents' wishes and developing my own identity. There came a point in time when I chose to develop my own identity, against my parents' wishes, by going across the road to the family that owned a grocery store. They were liberal, educated and had a lot of knowledge of the outside world. I saw a lot of books there I didn't know ever existed.

When I became aware that my teenage son was also searching for his identity, I discovered that he had different issues – one was his body image. At first I had difficulty with that because I had seen people in the concentration camps who were very physically depleted – their concern was how they were going stay alive and get their next piece of bread. As a parent, I set aside my difficulties because it was very important to support my son with whatever issues he had. I believed it would make it easier for him to find himself.

My desire for approval has motivated me to be a perfection-ist, and I tend to over-extend myself with every commitment I make. Regardless of how much energy it takes and the personal discomfort I feel, I need to outwork everybody else. And as often as my mother tries, she cannot convince me to slow down. She has always been fearful that I will hurt myself. Over the years, she had struggled with the thought of losing me because she had lost so much in the past, including her mother, father, siblings and the rest of her extended family in the Holocaust. And if that wasn't enough, she lost her twin daughter during childbirth and her husband from a senseless car accident. Because of these fears, my mother has always tried to protect me. She relied so heavily on her own determination and perseverance to survive, and after such great efforts to raise me well, felt responsible for ensuring my successes. I used to think that I needed to learn these lessons for myself as my mother did, but the truth of the matter is that no amount of determination and perseverance will enable individuals to achieve success on their own. People need other people – my mother and I need each other.

Research about body image suggests that about one-third of high-school boys actively attempt to gain body weight in order to be stronger, perform better at sports and attain a better body image. The plan involves heavy weightlifting and eating a high-calorie diet. It is an ego-driven process that involves getting on the scales regularly, in some cases multiple times a day, as well as checking out one's body shape in mirrors and every window reflection they pass. I was one of those boys.

When my father was still alive I was not allowed to participate in organized sports leagues. He particularly did not like the aggressive nature of hockey, so much so that he wouldn't even let me play road hockey. He was afraid I was going to hurt myself. My mother recalls how angry my father was after watching a hockey brawl between Sweden and Czechoslovakia. I'm sure this contributed to his dislike for the game and his decision not to let me play.

Though I was under the age of ten, I felt it was important to get involved just like the rest of my friends, who for the most part played hockey. They seemed so confident about their bodies and athletic abilities. I started to feel very insecure about the fact that they were experiencing real competition – and I was being left behind. I give my mother a lot of credit because she went to my dad and asked him in private to be a little more flexible – but he never relented. After my father had a serious car accident and became terminally ill, she took the risk and gave me an opportunity to join a local hockey team. I am thankful to this day for her believing in me. She had been denied many opportunities to experience life when she was growing up and I know she didn't want the same thing to happen to me.

When I was in Grade 9 I came home for lunch every day and my mother made me vegetable soup and cheese sandwiches. I would often arrive at the door crying because my friends had been bullying me about my big feet, big nose and skinny body. "The kids are telling me that I am different," I would say. And she would respond, "It's okay to be different; you don't have to look like one of the herd." That was one of the most important messages my mother gave me as I was growing up, and I have tried to pass it on to my own children.

I played basketball throughout high school, but regardless of my successes, I was never really satisfied with my accomplishments. I wasn't comfortable with the way my body looked, and I

still felt inferior to most of the other athletes my age. I was 6'3"
and pretty lean, but most of my friends had much more muscular physiques. They all played on the football team and were
involved in weight training to gain body weight – but I was too
shy to get involved with lifting weights. I was embarrassed about
my lack of strength and I couldn't bear to show my skinny body
to the other boys.

My mother's parents had also been concerned about her being so
skinny. They made her wear two pairs of bloomers and tried fat-
tening her up by feeding her extra food. They thought she might
not be appealing for marriage if she was skinny. I often think
about how strong my mother's body is. At age eighty-six she still
carries her own firewood. Given the physical abuse she endured
while in the concentration camps, it's amazing how physically
resilient she is.

After graduating from Grade 13 I decided to defer my acceptance to university for a year and hang around my hometown
and work. I was asked to coach one of the town's house-league
hockey teams by a gentleman named Vic. I really loved hockey

and the thought of working with young kids seemed like a lot of fun, so I took up the offer. At the time I had no idea how that decision would impact on my future.

Vic was forty-two years of age, solidly built and very confident in his manner. After arriving at the arena one day for practice I listened as he told me a story about how he used to be a competitive bodybuilder when he was a younger man. Then he remarked on my physical size and frame and suggested that I had the potential to be an excellent bodybuilder. He said that if I was interested he would like to get back into training with me. I was a little taken back by his personal observations and comments. I'm not sure I believed him, but my nature was (and still is today) to say to myself, "Here's an opportunity to do something different. Why not go for it?" Deep down I knew that Vic was offering me an opportunity I just couldn't resist. I have come to realize that what he offered me was support and trust.

Three nights a week I would drive twenty minutes out of town to the small village where Vic lived with his wife and kids. Down in the basement he had set up several old-style weight-training bars, plates and benches, which he had saved from his body-building days twenty years earlier. We started "pumping iron" in that dimly lit basement, on a moldy, damp, concrete floor, out of sight of anyone who might be inclined to laugh at me.

I quickly became fascinated by the whole experience of body-building and willingly immersed myself in the culture, which included reading bodybuilding magazines, consuming numerous supplements, creating special diets and studying the latest fads in training techniques. Though progress was slow, I was committed to seeing results and trained really hard. My mother took an interest in my health craze, supported my nutritional needs, and always had positive words of encouragement when I talked about my training. She allowed me to live at home rent-free; I didn't even have to help pay for my food. I knew she was giving me the freedom she hadn't experienced as a young adult.

A few of my buddies still lived in town after graduating from high school. One Saturday night we met at my closest friend's place before heading out to a party for the evening. When I arrived I was surprised to find a couple of guys there who had played on my high-school football team who were amazing athletes – the ones who were revered by all the other guys – and the girls too. I had been bodybuilding with Vic for about three months and could feel the changes happening in my body. I was pretty proud of the strength and size gains I was starting to see. For some reason I decided I wanted to show these guys the results of my new training program. I think I wanted to show them that I deserved to be accepted as one of them. I took my shirt off. They started to laugh and I was devastated.

After that totally embarrassing encounter I decided to increase my commitment to training, and lifting weights became my obsession for the next four years. I was angry and I took it out on those old weights down in Vic's stinky basement. I was consuming an incredible number of vitamin pills a day and eating like a horse. I got bigger and heavier – forty pounds heavier. Eventually, I set up my own training area in my mother's basement. She would come downstairs to help spot my lifts for me. She recognized that I was trying to improve my body image and could see that I was looking better and feeling more comfortable with who

I was. My mother never believed it was good enough to say to your child, "Just get over it." Although she never read to me, she always supported my interests and showed me that she trusted my judgment. Someone else could teach me to read, but no on else could show me such love. My mother continues to support my efforts to maintain a healthy body. It is not unusual for her to show up at my door with a bottle of vitamins that she believes will help improve my health.

I lacked self-confidence growing up, and my poor body image had a lot to do with that. I never understood why my friends couldn't – or wouldn't – support me when I was trying to do something to change the way I felt about myself. Were they not also seeking that kind of approval from others? Isn't everyone afraid, on some level, that they will not be accepted? Why is it that people choose to victimize others to make themselves feel better or more superior? My mother experienced the Nazis' attempt to victimize the Jews. As a result, she learned the value of acceptance, which she has taught me.

Sometimes a positive result can come from a negative action, particularly if you remain focused on your goal. When I decided to attend university I got involved in rowing and made a lot of great friends that I have kept over the past 30 years. Several years later, I taught physical education at the high-school level and developed a weight-training course for males and females that introduced them to a responsible way of improving health and fitness.

Over the years I pushed myself hard, always seeking the approval of others. I've driven my poor mother to worry and tears while she watched me do this. However, she often told me, "Until you truly love yourself, it's extremely difficult to accept others as they are, and be the person you are meant to be." She was right. What is hidden on the inside will always appear on the outside.

I learned from my mother that in order to feel good about oneself on the outside we have to accept who we are on the inside, and until we resolve our inner conflicts it will be difficult to move forward in a positive direction.

5

When you say, "I can't," you really mean, "I don't want to."

We arrived at Auschwitz-Birkenau on a cloudy morning on May 19, 1944. When the boxcar doors opened, we could see guard dogs, barbed wire, electric fences and high towers with machine guns and SS troops on them. People were relieved to be getting out of the box-cars, expecting to get food and water and a breath of fresh air, but there was no food and water for us, and the air was filled with an awful stench. One prisoner was shouting to cover what another prisoner was whispering to me: "Give the child to an older woman." I had my niece Judy with me and Mama had the other two, one in her arms and one hanging on her coat. I felt that he knew something and was trying to help me, so I gave my niece to Mama. These prisoners tried to save many young mothers and their children from being taken immediately to the gas chambers. They approached one young mother and her four-year-old son and told her what they had told me. In Hungarian, she asked why she should do this, and in the end she gave her child to her mother, who was standing with her. The little boy cried, "I don't want to go with my Bubba, I want to go with you!" These were the last words this mother heard from her child.

I have made many difficult decisions over my lifetime, but none as horrific as the decision that young mothers were faced with during the selection process at Auschwitz. How incredibly difficult it must have been to watch your family be taken to the gas chambers, as your life was saved by the decision to let go of your children.

I have discussed the topic of survival with my mother on many occasions. Because she has such a strong will and has faced so many obstacles, she has been a great source of inspiration and guidance for me as I navigate my own uncomfortable life situations. When

I ask my mother what it takes to survive the ups and downs of life she talks about what it was like to experience living hell in Auschwitz, and the importance of having a positive attitude, self-determination – and even believing in fate.

They made the men go in one line and the women in another, four or five in a row. The horrible smell around us reminded me of when we burned the last feathers off chickens after we plucked them. We stopped at the gate, where there was an officer with a little wand in his hand. This was the Angel of Death, Doctor Mengele. By pointing the wand, without saying a word, he indicated which direction each person was to go. In this way, he decided who would live and who would die.

At the gate my younger sister and I were sent to the right with other young women, while my two brothers and my brother-in-law were sent to the left with my father. My older brother Martin was a small person who had been born with one leg shorter than the other. It wasn't noticeable when he walked because he had orthopedic shoes. But when they stripped him nude they could tell, and I assume that he was sent immediately to the gas chambers. My sister-in-law and her baby went in another direction, along with my mother and her three grandchildren.

I think about the selection process quite often and reflect upon how fate had worked to save my life. In the year 2001, I was in Peterborough to speak at a local high school. A woman living there happened to hear me on television that morning. She decided to come and hear me speak to the students. That evening she came to the hotel where I was staying and brought with her some material she had printed off a website called "The Alphabet of Auschwitz." As I read through the pages of the website I came to the letter "D" for doctors. The link described the activities of the doctors at the camp during the selection process. It said that anyone who arrived with a scar from surgery was immediately sent to the gas chambers. The thought devastated me because I remembered my scar from my appendix operation one month before the Germans came to occupy our city in Hungary. After being sent to the right, our group of young women had approached the first buildings where we had to take our clothes off. We were stripped naked outside, in the open, with half a dozen SS officers looking at our bodies. There was still a red scar from my appendix operation in February so when I took my clothes off I hung them on my arm, covering the scar. I don't know why I did this, as most girls held their clothes in front of them, trying to cover themselves. However, this action saved my life, as they only wanted strong, physically fit workers, and I would have probably have been sent to the gas chambers if they had seen the scar.

Surviving the selection process was only the beginning of my journey of survival. With each passing moment I had to make another decision about what to say and when to keep quiet. Every day we got a cup of soup and a piece of dark bread, which was 70 percent sawdust. One day another prisoner and I were chosen to go to the kitchen to bring back the soup. On the way we had to pass what appeared to be a family camp, and the other prisoner and I wanted to talk through the barbed wire to the people but we were stopped immediately and told, "Do you want to go to the crematorium? We are already on the way there; it's not too far from the kitchen. In Auschwitz you don't speak to anyone and you don't cry or you are dead." They told us that these families behind the barbed wire were being used by Dr. Mengele for medical experiments and would later be exterminated.

We regularly passed the crematorium area, where there were dead bodies everywhere. There was always that sickening smell in the air and we could hear people screaming. At the time we didn't know why they were screaming, but we found out later that they were being herded into "bathhouses" to be executed. Once people were jammed in and the doors were closed, the chemical Zyclon B, mixed with other chemicals to produce cyanide gas, was pumped out of the shower-heads instead of water. This gas was heavy and settled near the floor at first, then worked its way up to the ceiling. This meant that every-body did not die at the same time. The young, the old and the sick were always closest to the floor. People gasping for air climbed on top of other people and bodies, and the pile got higher and higher. When the bathhouse doors were opened children were found with their heads crushed and their arms distended and dislocated. Sometimes those people nearest the roof were able to survive, but they were shot as soon as they were found.

My sister and I were among 2000 young female prisoners that were shipped from Auschwitz to Germany to work in a slave labour camp. It was a great relief to be taken away from Auschwitz and the smell of human flesh burning. A smaller group of women were taken from the original 2000 to another city in Germany, Essen, where we worked for a large ammunition factory. The Allies were bombing the area very heavily – they leveled the city to the ground. We were not allowed to go into the same shelter where the German civilians went during the air raids. Instead, the 520 women that I worked with shared four half-moon-shaped bunkers that were covered with grass. A group of 156 Ukrainians had arrived and took over one of the bunkers next to our camp for themselves. They were families – mothers, fathers and children – who came to work voluntarily in Germany. One night the bombing started and being creatures of habit we ran for all four of the bunkers. The Ukrainians wouldn't allow any of the Jewish prisoners to enter their bunker because of their strong anti-Semitic feelings, so the 520 of us crammed into the remaining three. We could hear the airplanes above us and the bombs falling. We didn't fear the bombs we heard – it's the one you don't hear that kills you. We also felt the air pressure change when they exploded. It was horrendous. After the air raid ended the SS came from their coalmine bunker and moved us back to our basement living quarters.

The next morning we lined up outside as we did every morning, to be counted to be sure no one had escaped. We saw that the bunker that the Ukrainian people had been in was gone. One bomb had hit it and all we had felt at the time was a change in the air pressure. Every one of those 156 people, men, women and children had been wiped out, right in the bunker. The SS and other Germans who had gone across to the coal mine said, "From here on in we'll go where the Yuden *(Jews) go." As it turned out the Ukrainians had done us a big favour. However, they were still human beings in spite of the fact that they hated us. I especially felt bad about the children because they were still innocent of the racist attitudes and anti-Semitic behaviour of their parents.*

One night I had to get out of the basement because I could not bring myself to pee on the straw. There was no light outside so I found myself crawling through the snow and the rubbish. I saw two people by the wall, a blonde woman wearing a white pantsuit and the SS commander of the camp. The woman was in her late 20s, a little older than I was, and she came from Sziget, the same town where my grandfather lived. I could only see her back as she was kneeling in front of him. He was a shrimp and couldn't have been more than five-feet tall. When I saw what they were doing I was petrified because I had never seen anything like that ever before – sex and lovemaking were never discussed in a Hasidic family – and I was afraid of being seen. She would have had no choice anyway. It was either sex or death, so she was wise to do what the SS commander wanted her to do. I remembered my Mama saying to me at the gates to Auschwitz: "Better they shoot you than touch you." In her mind it would be better for me to die than have somebody use me sexually. I disagree with that philosophy. I would have done the same thing as the woman in white. I believe this woman's sacrifice saved us from being shot that morning.

My mother walked a fine line between survival and death during her time in the death camps. Many of the victims of the Holocaust did not die from physical torture, starvation or disease; they were unable to hang on emotionally or spiritually. My mother survived by making smart decisions, having incredibly strong willpower – and being in the right place at the right time. After the camps, my mother's life was filled with personal struggle, mostly because of her lack of confidence, which she attributes to the severe putdowns she used to receive from her father. I asked her one day if she felt that her father's harsh treatment might have prepared her to face what she experienced in the camps, and she agreed it was possible. But, regardless of what she had experienced, she still needed a lot of encouragement to move forward in her life. I now know that most of her energy was focused on trying to raise me to be a kind, caring and responsible human being.

As a survivor, it is very important to focus on the meaning of life and what really matters. I have learned that having more things doesn't really improve the quality of one's life. What I need is more life. I have learned to prioritize and not take anything for granted.

In the early 1970s my mother and I built a cottage two hours north of Toronto and it was during our weekends up north that we would talk about my mother's goal of writing a book one day. I remember saying to her, "Mom, is this just talk?" She responded by saying, "No – but I don't know how to write." That was still her biggest fear, but I told her, "Don't worry Mom, you can learn how." The first of her three books was published in 2000 and has sold over 20,000 copies Canada-wide. I am very proud of my mother's determination to face and overcome her fears. She deserves all the recognition she receives.

My mother never wanted to fly. I encouraged her to get on a plane because I felt it was the best way for her to get across the country to spread her message of compassion and acceptance to more students. I kept saying to her, "Mom, you're going to be all right." For a number of years I encouraged my mother to return to her hometown and try to re-connect with her roots. She was adamant that she would never do it at her age. I told her "It takes courage to go back into the dark – but when it's all over and the day is done the sun will shine." Her trip to Hungary and the retracing of her Holocaust experience took place in the fall of 2007 and led to the creation of a second book and full-length documentary film.

For six years my mother travelled thousands of miles, mostly throughout Ontario, speaking to students. She felt very strongly that she had to give back to the community and spread her message of compassion and acceptance. She never charged a speaking fee or received any compensation for her out-of-pocket travel expenses. One day after her car finally broke down I asked my mother, "So now that your car is gone, where are you going to get the money to buy a new one?" My mother decided at that point that she would charge a nominal fee to cover her travel expenses.

I was pleased that my mother had decided to charge an honourarium. She did not work until I had finished high school, which resulted in her having very little income for many years. Despite this, she found a way to provide for my needs so that I could have the kinds of experiences that teenagers need to develop. She deserved to be compensated for her efforts. And the charging of a fee in no way deterred anyone from inviting her to speak.

After speaking at a high school in Owen Sound my mother was approached by a student who asked her the question, "What was it like as a Holocaust survivor to raise a son?"

It was very difficult because I had lost my family, my husband and my twin daughter. I was worried that I might also lose my son. When you have been deprived of many things in life or denied opportunity it is

When you say, "I can't," you really mean, "I don't want to."

very difficult to let go – but I needed to do this. Receiving encouragement from my son has meant everything to me and without it I might not be where I am today. The most important thing for me was to have an open mind to my son's suggestions. Very often we don't realize how much we can learn from our children.

I learned from my mother the importance of having a positive attitude and being grateful for the things we all have. She taught me the importance of making smart decisions, demonstrating strong willpower, and having faith that the best possible solution will appear when it is most needed. Sometimes, when I get down on myself, I need to take a close look at what my mother has overcome and accomplished, and remind myself of the importance of having a positive outlook on life.

6

We must be clear about what we choose to do, how we choose to do it, and where we are coming from when we choose to do it.

After being liberated from Bergen-Belsen I chose to be quarantined in Sweden, a country that had been neutral during World War II, and a place where people were known for their kindness. In October 1945 there was a dance in a small Swedish village where I lived and some of the girls decided to go and see what it was all about. They asked me to come along and I said I wasn't going to go because I had never danced with a boy; however they did persuade me to go. When we arrived at the large dance hall everybody was staring at us, the refugees. Our clothes weren't exactly the most elegant. We were dressed in a kind of sporty style, wearing skirts and blouses or whatever clothes they had given us. A young Swedish man named Rude asked me to dance. I wasn't a very good dancer, because when I was growing up, Hasidic girls didn't dance with boys. If we danced at a wedding or any other simcha (special occasion), we would dance with girls, so I was very nervous. However, I got my rhythm back and it felt nice to be dancing. Rude kept coming back and asking me to dance. At one point, he saw a girl coming into the hall and he went and spoke to her. I didn't know who she was, but she was dressed very well and was beautiful, with gorgeous long hair and white teeth. I couldn't speak Swedish so I couldn't ask him what that was all about. It wasn't that important to me at that time because I wasn't looking for a boyfriend. Later he told me that the girl at the door had become his ex-girlfriend that night.

Rude and I began seeing each other a couple of times a week. He was travelling by bus each day to Stockholm to attend the Technical Institute for Engineering and would invite me to spend Wednesday evenings with him at his family's home while he studied to be an engineer. At first I felt very uncomfortable because of my lack of education. During

> We must be clear about what we choose to do, how we choose to do it,
> and where we are coming from when we choose to do it.

one of our conversations I asked why he didn't have a well-educated Swedish girlfriend, and he replied, "You have more in your head than thirty Swedish girls put together." He made me realize that I had inner qualities and spiritual values, and I began to feel less uncomfortable within myself. He had enough insight to see beyond my education and appearance and our relationship grew from this point.

If there is one striking and unique aspect that defines our individuality, it is our physical appearance. Long before we give voice to our thoughts and emotions, we reveal our bodies to the world – and take the risk of being judged by others. And the way we choose to portray ourselves tells a whole lot about how we feel inside.

Imagine being a twenty-one year old woman arriving in a foreign country after being liberated from the Holocaust. A short time ago you were a shadow of a human waiting to be exterminated, and then suddenly, you are free to make life-choices for yourself. Having never before experienced an intimate relationship with a member of the opposite sex, you are faced with yet another challenge – how do you overcome the fear of intimacy?

While Rude studied, I embroidered a tablecloth. When he was finished he would walk me back to my apartment, which was in a dormitory in a wooded area. Our relationship became affectionate and I appreciated his patience. Perhaps he understood that my experiences in the camps had had a negative effect on my sexual feelings. However, he could not know that it went much deeper than that. In my home none of us saw each other half undressed, let alone naked. Sex was never discussed or referred to; sexuality was completely denied and it didn't exist until seven days before marriage. The unspoken message was that you should ignore your own body unless you cut yourself and were bleeding. I was free from the camps but not my childhood training I had received. I felt very inadequate and unsure of myself in social situations.

One day after I got home from work I decided to have a shower, so I undressed and put on my royal blue bathrobe. I left my apartment door ajar and when I returned to my apartment Rude was standing there. He had found the door open and when I did not answer he walked in. He untied the belt of my bathrobe and lifted me onto the bed standing up. I can still see the look on his face as he exposed my body. I was absolutely shocked when he told me I had a beautiful body and should be proud of it. No, nothing happened that time. We had a lot to discuss before anything did happen. My greatest fear was that if I had sex outside of marriage Rude would think I was a "bad woman" and would leave me. He had great difficulty understanding that my fear of sexual matters stemmed from my childhood training by my family. I couldn't tell him that one night when I was fifteen, I was sleeping in a bed beside my mother when my father returned from a trip, came into the room and proceeded to have sex with my mother. I lay there awake, confused and frightened, not knowing what was happening, as we had been given no sex education at all. Two of the other children were sleeping in another bed in the same room. I still wonder how my parents could have been so insensitive to the fact that children were in the room and might hear and see them.

As a Swede, Rude could see nothing wrong with two people loving each other and making love. Sometime later, before we became intimate, I was visiting his home on a cold winter night and his mother suggested I stay overnight. I accepted and she made up the sofa bed for two. Rude quietly said to his mom, "Eva and I have yet to sleep *together." Rude taught me to open my mind to a new and better way of living. He taught me that it was okay to express myself sexually and to feel good about and love my body. Of course, that can only begin to happen when you love yourself. My experience in the camps had shut down all possibility of those feelings in me, but Rude's love for me helped to open them up again. Through his caring, tender, loving presence I began to love myself and allow myself to experience what I had never dreamed was possible.*

My mother was so fortunate to have met a man like my father after being dehumanized in the camps. My father recognized her spiritual qualities, and as a result, she learned self-respect and became an incredibly trusting individual. My mother allowed herself to be vulnerable in her relationship with my father and a strong and loving bond was formed between them. My mother has lived her whole life this way.

After my father passed away my mother tried to nurture the same qualities in her relationships with other men, but she was unsuccessful. Being a teenager, I didn't realize how difficult it was for her to lose my father or why she continued to place herself in such a vulnerable position over and over again. Now I understand how easy it can be to feel lonely when we aren't connecting with the right person. In my own life, I have also made some poor decisions when I wasn't clear about where I was coming from. It's so important to be clear in our own mind about the choices we are about to make – and the potential consequences of those choices.

We don't need to be fat, skinny, short or tall, or have experienced the Holocaust, to feel insecure about the way we look or who we are. The average female in North America is five-foot-four inches tall and weighs one hundred and forty pounds. The average model is five-foot-eleven inches tall and weighs one hundred and seventeen pounds – but only three percent of females actually fit that description. Still, virtually every young female worries about her physical appearance and how her peer group, including boys, will accept her. It's no better for males as they try to live up to the media's image of the perfectly chiseled and muscular body.

I remember working with a young female athlete a number of

years ago who developed anorexia while training for long-distance running. She was a very bright and talented athlete and student. She had tremendous physical attributes and abilities – not to mention her obviously outstanding level of fitness. By everyone else's standards she had the perfect body. But it wasn't the way she saw it. In an attempt to feel better about her appearance she chose to adopt an unrealistic training schedule and dietary plan that eventually became overly demanding. After developing a serious illness, she and her family finally came to realize that something was out of balance.

Coping with our own insecurities and fears tugs at our self-confidence from the time we enter kindergarten. We want to love and accept who we are – but often rely on our friends and acquaintances to help us find ourselves. Our search becomes defined by our behaviours – the way we dress, what we consume, the activities we choose to opt in or out of, and the risks we are willing to take – particularly those risks that involve sharing our bodies intimately with others. My mother taught me to have the utmost respect for my partner. The caring and devoted

> We must be clear about what we choose to do, how we choose to do it,
> and where we are coming from when we choose to do it.

relationship that my mother experienced with my father provided me with a positive role model.

I learned from my mother that what we choose to do, and how we choose to do it, is a reflection of how comfortable we are with ourselves. When we are clear about our own inner qualities we will be less likely to place ourselves in a position that may not be in our best interest – particularly when we are feeling lonely.

7

Certain behaviours have predictable outcomes.

When I was a child I was sent alone to my uncle's egg-grading station to get cracked eggs. I was really frightened to go into his building because it was really dark in there. I was afraid of the dark; Mama used to warn us not to go out in the dark because the Tartars (Mongolian people) would steal us away from her. I enjoyed going to the open market because there were lots of things to see there – people, poultry, fruit and vegetables, flowers, dry goods and even wood for the stove. One Friday evening before my father came home from the synagogue, when I was about ten, two or three of us were watching a trapeze artist on a high wire in the market square. As we stood there hypnotized I turned around and saw my father. He had been out looking for us because it was wrong to go out Friday after sundown. We did not get spanked until Saturday night or Sunday morning and even today I do not understand why a child should have to wait 24 to 48 hours in fear of a future spanking. Today I see that this kind of behaviour was sadistic and I cannot see any positive side to it. My father felt that his action was justified because we were late for supper. The fact that we had never seen a trapeze act before and had lost track of time was no excuse. I was never even given a chance to explain.

When I was sixteen years old I confronted my father for the first time. He arrived home at noon from the synagogue and was telling my mother a tragic story about a Jewish family whose daughter and her gentile boyfriend were found shot dead in a cornfield. My father was very upset by this tragic event. I felt he should not be discussing this incident in front of the children and I confronted him, saying, "It's not up to us to talk about other people's problems." He was shocked into silence at my remarks. But what angered me most was that two young people were dead because they loved each other and their parents' religious beliefs got in the way. The girl's parents would not accept the gentile boyfriend. So the couple saw suicide as their only option. My father must have sensed that my attitude was maturing in a different direction than he would have liked. He became more suspicious of my different beliefs about freedom and privacy, and my growing independence.

In 1942 my brother-in-law needed a piece of paper to prove that his grandfather had paid tax, so I was sent on a seven-hour train trip to Debrecen at the age of seventeen. This was only my second trip out of town. I was to stay with an Orthodox Jewish family who owned a delicatessen and would provide my meals. The first evening I was there I went out, and the feeling of freedom, of being on my own, was overwhelming. I looked for a bus and asked the driver where there was a movie theatre. He told me to go to the end of the line to the Opera House. I don't remember the name of the movie but I do remember the story. I especially remember the love scene in the swimming pool by the garden. Being so young and naïve I had never been in the situation myself, but it was thrilling to watch. I went straight back to my room afterwards, fantasizing and thinking about all the beautiful love scenes. This experience at the theatre hit me like a lightning bolt, and stimulated emotions and physical sensations that were all new to me. I wished I had someone to hug and kiss and make love to me that way. Although I asked myself why I had these feelings and wondered if they were normal, I knew that I liked these feelings very much. Why wasn't I told that girls could have these feelings and taught how to deal with them? These feelings did not last, but the memory of them did. Of course I could not share this experience with my mother or sisters. We were never exposed to romantic love because Hasidic marriages are arranged without love entering the picture. Perhaps love comes later for them, I don't know. It was probably fortunate that no male companion was involved in my movie experience because I would have been completely vulnerable to his advances. It is said that ignorance is bliss but in this instance my ignorance could have caused a disaster: pregnancy and being denounced by my family.

The next morning, after I picked up my brother-in-law's papers at the Registry Office, I took the train home. My father called me outside and confronted me with information about what I had been doing while I was away. He must have gone to the post office, telephoned the people with whom I stayed and had them spy on me. He hit me, slapped me in the face, verbally abused me, and kicked me with his boots. He always wore knee-high leather boots with his black trousers tucked in them. It was very degrading to be beaten in such a way and I felt I was going to collapse. I denied doing any wrong, never admitting to him that I had gone to a movie. The beating went on for about two hours, outside in the yard behind a fence where we couldn't be seen. I have asked myself many times why he beat me in the yard and not inside the house. Obviously he did not want to discipline me in front of my siblings. I had been spanked many times inside the house, often being hit with his belt while lying across his lap, but this was a much more vicious beating and it took place outside the house. Could it be that he wanted to maintain a gentle father image with my siblings? Could it be he feared his other children would lose faith in his teachings? It went on until my mother opened the door and said, "Haim Ytzhog, enough. This is enough now."

My mother taught me a lot of things, some positive and some negative. She taught me to be resourceful, how to be a good homemaker, how to cook and bake. I saw how caring she was, especially when she made pretty dresses for us. She was a very devoted person. The one negative trait that stands out in my mind was her inability or unwillingness to discipline us when she felt we needed it. The fact that my mother was unwell from the time I was born, and had six children to look after, made it difficult for her to take on the responsibility of disciplining. If my father were out of town for four or five weeks we would have to wait for his return to be punished. I got to the point that I used to fear my father's return and view him as a villain. Sometimes I even wished that he would never come back. I resented my mother's decision not to deal with me promptly because it made me feel so negative towards my father. Her behaviour also demonstrated to us that she was a weaker parent than my father.

I recall only one time that I was spanked by my father. I don't remember what I did to make him so angry. He ushered me into the bedroom and ordered me to pull my pants down while he took his belt off. I remember the feeling of terror as I watched and anticipated what was to come next. He hit me only three times. I will never forget it. From that point forward I was fearful of the potential consequences I might receive if I did something wrong. I would never challenge him again during the short time we were together before his car accident.

Years ago parents recognized the importance of modelling appropriate behaviour for their children. The expectations were clearer, and the opportunities to challenge the reasoning behind those expectations were far more limited. You did what you were told. My mother's upbringing as a young teenager in Hungary provides an incredible contrast to the way parents discipline their children today. Religion and fear were the basis of her parents' teaching and it was accompanied by anger and aggression. Because my mother chose not to follow his strict religious beliefs, her father felt disappointment, and believed he had failed to control her. In contrast, my mother chose to guide me by disciplining me in a caring and supportive way.

Several years ago, I was looking outside my office window toward the patio at the front of the school and witnessed a student violently kicking the doors leading into the cafeteria. As I looked closer, I noticed something hanging from the door. It appeared to be the carcass of an animal. It actually turned out to be the hindquarters of a deer. Three senior students, who were skipping class, had been out in the bush on a trail ride in their pickup truck. They had come across a deer carcass – the remains of a wolf kill. They decided to load the carcass into the back of their pickup truck and bring it to school to play a practical joke. They used the legs of the deer to barricade the cafeteria doors so that no one could get out of the building. News of the event spread quickly throughout the school. Teachers and students were at my office door sharing their disgust. Fortunately, students were more than willing to come forward with information about how this situation had come about.

This story describes one of the most unusual and disturbing events I had witnessed as a high-school administrator. The climate of the school was always my highest priority, and I felt it was important to keep examining which behaviours were appropriate and how to best respond to those which were not. In terms of consequences, the solution to the deer carcass incident seemed pretty straightforward to me. Each student responsible for bringing the dead animal parts to the school, and those students who helped barricade the door, would be suspended. A letter of apology would provide a certain measure of reconciliation towards the staff and students who were offended by the action. Assigning some community service hours with the custodians who had to clean up the mess, or with wildlife officials also seemed appropriate. However, in this particular situation, most of the parents of the offending students were not supportive of these measures. They did not view the actions of their children as being indicative of poor character or creating a potential health or safety risk to others in the building. In their minds, the fact that we lived in a northern community made it acceptable to transport dead animals to school. I saw no logic in their argument. The parents' lack of support made for some challenging discussion. Regardless, the consequences were levied and the rules of civility for our school were reinforced. In this situation, the parents showed a lack of support for what the education system was trying to achieve in terms of developing good citizens. The deer carcass story provides a good example of how differently parents can model expectations for their children. Since that incident I have asked myself many times, "How can we expect anything different from the children of such an environment?"

We all come from diverse backgrounds and many of us have experienced growing up in an unstable home environment. Teenagers are empowered by their access and control over the information that they receive through the World Wide Web and cell phones. Today's youth are often more informed than their parents about world issues and are able to make decisions about how they want to use their knowledge without the need or benefit of considering their parents' wisdom. Yet surely, no matter what generation we come from, our goal must be to learn that we are responsible for our own behaviour and for the choices that we make. For every one of our behaviours there is a consequence.

I wanted to be sure that my own children understood what expectations I had for them. I would describe my disciplining style as a mixture of both my mother's and father's. On one hand I was very rigid and controlling like my father. I remember my father spanking me and grew up believing it was right for him to use that form of discipline. On the other hand, I experienced my mother disciplining me as a single parent, and she demonstrated incredible patience and understanding toward the mistakes I made as a teenager. She felt that children should be disciplined with compassion and love and that disciplining with anger was ineffective. As my children grew older I realized how ineffective my harshness had been and made a greater effort to use a more caring approach to guiding them – much like my mother had used with me. I hope my children will make the right choices about disciplining when they have children.

The world is changing quickly and teenagers don't see the world the way their parents did when they were growing up. To learn the difference between right and wrong, teenagers must experience life as it is for them, without being shielded from the outside world. Open discussions about sex, relationships, discrimination, bullying and compassion are part of a trusting and caring relationship between a parent and child. Only by establishing this level of communication can parents successfully guide the growth and development of their children. This was the form of parenting that my mother used as a single parent, and I admire the level of patience that she demonstrated when discussing the issues that were affecting my development.

I learned from my mother that we are responsible for our own behaviour and the choices that we make – and we must consider the potential consequences before we take action. Different parents will have varying expectations for their children; however, they also have a responsibility to guide their children with an understanding and caring voice of reason.

Certain behaviours have predictable outcomes.

8

Every path has its puddle.

It was the week before liberation from Bergen-Belsen. I lived minute-by-minute and each day became an eternity. As the days went by we became more and more numb, weak from lack of food and water. I don't think anyone can imagine or understand the shock that witnessing such horrific conditions can have on the mind. I was afraid to lie down for fear I might not get up, afraid to sit down because I might be eaten by the lice, and afraid to stand up for fear I'd fall down. I found out later there had been cannibalism there and in Auschwitz too. It is really mind-boggling to think of those diseased bodies being eaten by dying prisoners, but it shows how human beings can be dehumanized to the point where they'll do anything for survival. To eat human flesh, one must have lost all faith and hope. We saw hills of dead bodies and skeletons lying on top of each other, mountains of them. Once I saw a young face in the pile of bodies. All the other bodies were skeletons but her face was still young and beautiful. I still wonder how she came to be on that pile, as she was the only one who was not a skeleton. Perhaps she was raped and then shot.

Eventually I fell ill with typhoid fever. No matter how sick we were, we were supposed to be counted, but there were days I couldn't do it. I had a high fever and just lay among the dead bodies on the floor, covered with lice. Walking skeletons and human waste filled the barracks. Most of the other prisoners had dysentery (non-stop diarrhea), but I had the opposite problem. For ten days I couldn't go to the bathroom. Of course the body needs food before it can produce waste, and we were barely getting starvation rations. Then six days before the Allies arrived the SS shut off the water completely and took away our food rations. Perhaps they felt that without food or water we would all die, and many did. Many prisoners were just skin and bones, their eyes bulging out of their sunken bodies, barely recognizable as humans. They died and fell to the floor or on the ground.

At that point I was too sick to care what was happening or think about what the outcome would be. I was so hot with fever that I peed on a rag and put it on my head, hoping it might cool me down. However, we were all suffering from dehydration too, so not much fluid came out of me. One morning I was too sick to go outside and be counted and the girls stood for several hours waiting to be counted. Some of the girls collapsed and were dragged into the barracks. About two hours later the rest of the girls came back in and told me that the SS guards had left and come back with white bands on their arms. They had surrendered to the Allies.

We do not always get to choose our path, but fortunately most of us are often given that opportunity. I have had difficulty making decisions about my own path; however, because I respected my mother's opinions, I would often go to her for advice. I started confiding in her more frequently after I got married and the children were born. My first daughter, Brenna, arrived soon after my wife and I had gotten married. My career in teaching was two years old, and my struggles with ulcerative colitis and the spontaneous rupture of my spleen had become a preoccupation around the house. Career, parenting, marriage and health: four common areas of responsibility that I struggled with over a 25-year period. I've had some personal challenges to overcome, made some poor decisions along the way, and struggled to define what it means to be happy. Over those 25 years I would visit with my mother, looking for a sympathetic ear and hoping for support – I often came away feeling like I received neither.

My mother has always had an answer for each of my problems – her number one solution to almost any problem, is to change one's attitude. This has become such a predominant theme in our discussions that I have labeled her response the "positive attitude to the point of having a martyr-complex." I use the term martyr-complex because I feel like I'm supposed to overcome my suffering by remaining positive at all costs, regardless of how undesirable my situation is. I recognize the adversity that my mother faced being in a concentration camp and I accept that her survival is a testament to her positive attitude. However,

Every path has its puddle.

I keep reminding her that she was free to choose her attitude, but she didn't decide to be put in a concentration camp. On the other hand, I have an opportunity to make my own decisions about how to live my life. I have two choices when it comes to making a positive change; one choice is to change my attitude and the other is to change the experience. The fact is, I was not really suffering. I just kept making poor decisions that were creating puddles along my path – and I didn't want to take responsibility for what was happening.

The conversations with my mother became shorter and shorter as the years went by. I would confide in her about my problems, and she would try to give me her heartfelt opinion on what I needed to do to solve them. I didn't always agree with her suggestions, so I would challenge her response. Before sharing her views she would often say, "I know I shouldn't say anything" or sometimes she would say, "I'm just going to say something in response to what you said the other day and then I'm going to be quiet." It really bothered me when she would say that. I started visiting less and less and staying for shorter periods of time.

We both knew the tensions were mounting but we couldn't seem to get past our differing views. I was looking for comfort where she was offering solutions.

One of the big issues for many years was my interest in moving to the west coast of Canada. The West holds a special place in my heart when I am there; it's like being at home. For a number of years I looked for a teaching job out there and tried to talk my family, including my mother, into moving if I found a job; however, no one ever shared my interest.

Jan seemed to be thinking, "She's trying to control my life." I never told him not to change his lifestyle. When he wanted to go and live out west I said to him, "You have my blessing." Under no circumstances did I ever say to him "Don't go here or don't go there." He was free to make his choices and I didn't make them for him. For some young adults it's difficult to separate reality from perception. I didn't tell my son to take the job at the local school board. When he had issues with co-workers fresh out of university, and wanted to change the whole education system, I did say to him, "Maybe you need to change your attitude. No matter where you are going to work, whether you are a doctor, lawyer, or any other profession, we must allow space between co-workers – meaning one person's ideas are not always the right ones."

My understanding today is that my son didn't want to hear me say, "Change your attitude." Perhaps what he might have wanted to hear was, "Oh you poor boy – you should quit your job." Unfortunately, I could not be a hypocrite and say one thing and mean something else. So my son's perception at that time was that I didn't support him, and if I didn't support him then I didn't care. Nothing could be farther from the truth.

Later on, I realized that my mother did care, and I also became aware that there are many other people who do care. I had to make some adjustments in my thinking and be sure of my expectations, particularly as I became an administrator. One of the first issues I tackled was the throwing of food and garbage throughout the school. It was an important problem for me that related to my experiences as an elementary student.

I attended a very small public school until Grade 6, and then unexpectedly, I was transferred to a senior public school to complete Grades 7 and 8. When I first arrived with my classmates we were all very intimidated by the size of the new school and unfamiliar surroundings. The worst part of the experience was the lunch period. We had been used to having our lunch in our own classroom. At the new school everyone ate together in a large cafeteria where two or three teachers were assigned to supervise. Each day my mother would prepare my favourite lunch, which consisted of a thermos of hot soup and a cheese sandwich. I was always starving by lunch but felt very uncomfortable eating with all of the other students around me; this was because the cafeteria was out of control. Students threw food and sometimes it would land right in my thermos of soup, and that would be the end of my lunch for that day. The fact that students would throw their food and squish sandwiches they didn't like really bothered me. Seeing food on the floor made me feel sick to my stomach. By the time I graduated from senior public school and started high school I was able to walk home for lunch to enjoy my soup and sandwiches in the privacy of my own home.

As I was growing up my mother taught me to be thankful for the food I was given. I watched her create incredible soups from the bones and feet of chickens. Leftover mashed potatoes, eggs and onions were combined to make tasty potato latkes. Our small backyard garden was a source of fresh cucumbers, tomatoes, strawberries, zucchinis, onions and carrots. I used to help my mother prepare some of the meals. Nothing was wasted.

It was after a long stretch as a classroom teacher that I became a high-school administrator. The student population was 1150; however, our cafeteria only seated 278 students at one sitting. Many students would go off campus for lunch, so overcrowding in the cafeteria only became a problem during the winter months. The rule that was in place for many years prior to my arrival was that there was no eating or drinking in the hallways. Yet I noticed my first few days as vice-principal that most staff and students ate and drank in the halls – in spite of the fact that signs were clearly posted stating "No Eating or Drinking in the Halls." Garbage was everywhere and the floor was a mess. Food was smeared on the walls, lockers, benches, and on the hand railings in the stairwells. The staff complained that somebody had to do something about it. When I spoke to the custodial staff they made it abundantly clear that they didn't feel it was their responsibility to clean up the mess that others had deliberately made. Students were not willing to take responsibility for breaking the rules or cleaning up their own mess. So I asked myself, "Jan, what do you want to do about this situation?"

My fellow vice-principal felt very strongly that we had to do something about the lunch problem in our school. I remembered growing up with this real dislike for situations where food was being wasted. I knew I had a responsibility to help change the attitudes of our students. At first, we tried using the announcements to encourage students not to eat in the halls. Our personal appeal had little impact on their behaviour, so we started putting the student who threw food on the end of a broom or mop and made them clean the hallways. Students were suspended for throwing garbage or food down the stairwells. But things didn't get any better.

After several weeks, we decided to do a couple of things

differently. First, we convinced our principal to take down the signs forbidding eating or drinking in the halls. We announced to the students that eating would be allowed, but asked that they "please use the garbage cans provided." Extra garbage cans were placed on each floor within easy access of benches in the hall. At the end of each lunch hour the two of us would open up the custodial closet, pull out a broom, dustpan and wet mop, and together, clean the hallways of our school.

The first reaction from everyone was laughter. Then students began to make comments like, "Hey, Mr. Olsson, you're really good at that!" They would ask questions like, "Are you getting paid to do that?" A staff member who wanted to discuss the morality of my efforts challenged me. There was talk of legal action against me for doing the work of the custodians. I listened but continued modeling the behaviour I expected from others.

Slowly but surely, I began to notice a difference in the halls. Over the next three years I continued to model the behaviour that I was looking for in the students and the staff. It was in the spring of the fourth year that I realized the power of my actions. I had just come up the stairwell and walked back into the hallway when I noticed a teacher at the far end of the hallway. The teacher was bending down to pick up a piece of garbage. Later that day, I went to pick some garbage up that was close to where a group of students was standing and a student said, "That's okay, Mr. Olsson; don't worry about that – I'll get it for you." A similar situation, also involving students, happened twice more that day. Garbage cans were starting to get filled up and the halls were beginning to look much better. Teachers were starting to comment on the improvements that they were seeing. The custodians began supporting the effort. Modelling had started to influence the behaviour of others.

I had experienced a number of different emotions during my first four years at the school, including frustration, guilt, and even embarrassment at times. I couldn't understand why people had gotten so angry or why they were making fun of me. The first question I asked myself after all of this was, "Why did it take so long to reach my goal?" Then I wondered if I had been foolish to believe I was on the right path, and that everyone else would just follow my lead. My mistake was that I assumed everyone else would see it as I did. I learned from this experience that it wasn't as important to have others believe in what I was doing, as it was for me to believe in what I was doing. Once I understood this for myself, I was much more willing to accept the path I had chosen for myself, and better prepared to face the obstacles that I would encounter as part of my journey without trying to convince others that my path was the best one.

When speaking to students I remind them that the path they choose may have consequences for the rest of their life. I call it "the hard road and the hard road." I tell them that if they choose a path that requires little effort, like skipping class and not completing assignments, their life will likely become harder in the future, because they might have to settle for a job with poorer pay and working conditions. If they choose the hard path now, by having the self-discipline to go to class and complete their homework each night, they will be rewarded in the future with lifestyle opportunities that an uneducated person may not have access to. Either way there is a price to be paid. Each path has its puddles and we can't expect to reach our goal without facing them at some point along our journey.

My mother always says, "You choose your attitude." She experienced a journey that she did not choose to make; however, she did choose how she would respond to each situation she was in. It took me a long time to appreciate her message that every path has its puddle so choose your path wisely and expect to experience challenges along the way.

I learned from my mother the importance of perseverance and determination, and how our attitude can lead us to success or failure. It begins by increasing our ability to separate perception from reality, and then focusing our energy on the decisions we have in front of us.

Every path has its puddles.

9

Most of our strengths and weaknesses are self-determined.

After my son finished Grade 13 he applied to several universities. He was accepted, but decided to take a year off to work as a law clerk with a small law firm in Bradford, Ontario. He was very well received and they suggested to him that he attend law school. The next fall Jan enrolled in a Law Clerk course at a community college in Toronto but only lasted a couple of months. One night he came home and told me, "If I am going to be a family man I don't want to be a lawyer." So in the fall of 1976 three of my son's friends decided to travel to Western Canada for a year – and Jan decided to join them. I couldn't tell my *son to not go; however, I wasn't very happy about it because that old fear kept creeping in from all of my previous losses and the thought of having a long-distance relationship with him was painful. It was really my weakness and I had to accept that my son was leaving home for the first time at the age of twenty-two. I told myself that this is my son's life, and his journey, and I have to accept that. It took six weeks for the boys to travel across the country. Jan got a job in Vancouver but there wasn't much future in pumping gas for $3.50 per hour, so by April he was back home in Ontario trying to get accepted into university again.*

That summer I worked at five different jobs hoping to make enough money to pay for my education. I got a job driving a delivery truck but was fired because I was too slow finding the businesses where I was supposed to make the deliveries. My second job was at an insulation factory where I sat on a pile of telephone books all day long ripping them apart with my hands and throwing the chunks of pages into a shredder. I quit after one week. During the summer I applied to Trent University in Peterborough, Ontario, and based on my interview was given admission to the Psychology program.

On September 10, 1977, my mother dropped me off at the university for my first year of classes. I was about to turn twenty-three and I was a bit nervous at the thought of being with a lot of younger teenagers who had just graduated from high school. I went out to the pub that night hoping to meet some new friends. I was determined to get involved. While at the pub, four second-year students approached me and insisted I show up for the rowing team tryouts the following morning. I had been bodybuilding and running and felt like this was the challenge I had been looking for. I used to be a basketball player but the thought of trying a new sport that required a lot of strength appealed to me. I arrived at the boathouse at six a.m. the next morning with 45 other guys, and that was the beginning of a 25-year association with rowing as an athlete, coach, administrator and builder.

The training regime that I maintained over the next four years was extremely gruelling. It included 14 workouts each week and up to 30 hours of training, on and off the water. I consumed a very high-calorie diet, including the intake of numerous vitamin pills to help me maintain my body weight and support the energy requirements needed for those workouts. It was difficult to consume all of the calories between my workouts and avoid training on a full stomach, but I stuck to the plan religiously throughout my years of competitive rowing.

My rowing career had ended by the time I arrived at the Faculty of Education at Queen's University in 1981. I was still lifting weights, running and playing hockey to stay in shape, but had begun to notice that my digestive system was frequently upset – symptoms that I chose to disregard. In the spring of 1982 I was in Ottawa preparing to run the first of the three marathons that I would eventually run, and it was there that I first noticed blood in my bowel movement. A colonoscopy revealed that I had ulcerative colitis and my battle with the disease began.

One beautiful Sunday morning in 1985 I decided to go out for a short run. On this particular morning, I should have been running in my fourth marathon; however about three weeks earlier I decided not to race because I hadn't been feeling very well. After each run I felt sick. My fingertips and lips would get tingly and numb, and I always felt exhausted. These symptoms had persisted for several months but I had been ignoring them, just like I ignored the aches, pains and minor injuries I often experienced while training as a rower.

My wife and I, and our baby daughter, lived out in the country, about a fifteen-minute car ride from the small town of Gravenhurst Ontario. I chose an old logging road close to our small bungalow as the route for my two-mile run. I had looked upon it as somewhat of a ceremonial event given my absence from the actual race. When I arrived home after the run I was pleasantly surprised by how good I was feeling, figuring the three-week layoff had given me the rest I needed to recover from my sickness. I came into the house aiming to finish my workout with a few pushups and sit-ups. The pushups went just fine; however after my second sit-up I felt a sharp, stabbing pain in the left side of my abdomen. I knew right away that something was seriously wrong. I couldn't breathe or get myself up off the floor.

With baby in tow, and myself barely able to stay conscious, my wife drove 95 miles-per-hour down the highway to the regional hospital in Orillia. By the time I arrived my blood pressure had fallen to 70 over 50 and the doctors figured there must have been a leak somewhere inside of my abdomen. The plan was to take an x-ray and then do an exploratory procedure to see if there was any fluid buildup in my abdominal cavity. The x-ray showed that my spleen was six times its normal size, so the doctors undertook emergency measures to get me into the operating room to remove my spleen.

I had never been in a hospital for treatment before. The prep for surgery was quick. They got me into a gown, I signed a permission form, and then shortly after they gave me a sedative to knock me out for the operation. On the way to the operating room my spleen ruptured. The next thing I remember is waking up in intensive care with an incision that was five times the size normally used to remove a spleen. It was ugly and painful, but I had survived – according to the surgeon, by a margin of ten minutes.

It wasn't until after my spleen had ruptured that I really made a concerted effort to try and resolve the colitis problem. During my recovery time I realized that my bowels had cleared up.

The bleeding was gone and my stools had returned to normal. This led me to think that diet might have been a factor in the onset of the disease. I had overloaded my digestive system for so many years but then after not eating for a week, things were finally improving. I have never been a big supporter of the western medical model, though I am grateful for the doctors who saved my life. When my internal medicine doctor encouraged me to have part of my bowel removed to resolve the colitis, I chose to explore alternative holistic medicine.

It took 15 years to figure out exactly what combination of foods and which food allergies were causing the stresses on my digestive system. It was a difficult time. I tried all kinds of unusual remedies to heal my gut, including colonics, drinking clay, squishing grapes on my stomach and fasting for days on end. One time I fasted for eight days, consuming only distilled water. At times I was losing upwards of half a cup of blood a day, but I was determined to find a solution without the doctors having to remove my bowel. Depending on my health, my body weight would fluctuate dramatically. In the end, it was a little book that someone recommended to me that provided the answers to my problem. I was lucky – I could have done some serious damage to myself trying to fix the problem on my own – but I fixed it.

It wasn't the rowing that was the problem – it was the way I pushed myself so hard and overloaded my system. My mother had a lot of difficulty watching me suffer and didn't agree with what I was doing to myself. Throughout my years of health difficulties she continued to warn me about the consequences of my lifestyle. Regardless, my mother remained committed to supporting me regardless of all the negative choices I was making. She made special meals for me and purchased supplements and often helped carry the workload around the house by babysitting my children. My mother kept trying to tell me that I needed to accept myself and not always strive to be number one.

Perhaps I inherited my mother's strong determination and perseverance and this is what gave me the strength to push myself when others might have given up. But sometime our strengths can become our weakness, particularly if we do not keep our efforts in balance. Now I am using my determination to improve my physical health.

I learned from my mother the value of doing things in moderation. Sometimes our fears motivate us to push ourselves beyond our resources. We need to listen to our heart, mind and body so that we don't create suffering for ourselves.

10

If someone throws a stone at you,
you throw back a piece of bread.

I went to visit a high school in southern Ontario where I was asked to give two presentations back-to-back. I was about half way through my first presentation when I noticed somebody approaching the principal. A few words were exchanged and both individuals left the gymnasium.

I finished the first assembly and about five or ten minutes later the next group of students began to arrive with their teachers for the second assembly. The first teacher who came into the gymnasium asked me if I had heard what had happened and I said "no." She wasn't going to tell but said to me, "The principal will tell you later what happened this morning." At that point I had a feeling it was something serious. When the second assembly was about to begin I noticed the principal standing right beside a student who was sitting in a chair – the principal never left that position for the whole assembly. I started out my presentation by saying, "I am not here to judge anyone; I'm here to bring awareness of the power of hate. On the screen you will have an opportunity to see what hate did, and still does."

During lunch the principal told me what had happened that morning. A group of bullies, six senior male students, had decided that after I finished my second presentation they were going to come up on stage and salute me with "Heil Hitler." A female student in the hallway, who was a new Canadian, overheard the bullies talking about how they were going to carry this out and she decided she wasn't going to be a bystander. She was the one who went to the principal to report what she had heard. The organizers of the bullies were first-generation Canadians. The others involved were as well. When the principal approached them to say, "Your families also came from another country," they responded by saying, "That was different." The principal felt *that the students believed they were more valuable as human beings than I was. One of the students was not known as a bully in the school – he had been sucked in. He explained to the principal that he had told the others, "You can't do this – this is an old lady – she could die of a heart attack" – and the other five replied "so what?"*

I was called back to the same school to do another assembly the following year. At first I was reluctant to do it. Eventually I did accept the invitation because I remembered what my mother used to say: "If someone throws a stone at you, you throw back a piece of bread." I asked myself, "What do these students need and how can the staff, students and administration get these students involved in a positive way?" I wanted to be a part of the solution and that is why I chose to return to that school to speak. When I returned to give my presentation those boys were part of the assembly, and I was pleased to have the opportunity to show them that I was not angered by their intentions the previous year.

My mother tried to teach me to be kind and caring towards others. I was never a bully, but I was often bullied. One particular incident occurred when I was a teenager that involved a very close friend of mine, Bill. We were playing road hockey on the street right in front of his house where we often played for hours on the weekends. Bill and I were alone together that day, just "taking shots" on each other in net. We got into a bit of a disagreement about the rules of the game, and he decided he wasn't going to play any longer. He grabbed his stuff and headed for the front door of his house. I was so upset that he didn't want to play that I followed him to his front door and started calling him names. I called him a sissy. Name-calling is something I had never gotten into with my friends, or anyone else for that matter, and at that point I was quickly reminded of why I was afraid to do it. In the blink-of-an-eye Bill turned around and pushed me to the ground. He was so angered and physically aggressive that I was completely taken by surprise. Before I could protect myself he had me on my back on the concrete sidewalk that led to his front door. He was sitting on top of my chest with his knees pinning my arms to my side. He threatened to punch me in the face. I remember begging him to let me up while promising to never say a nasty word to him ever again – and he did.

If someone throws a stone at you, you throw back a piece of bread.

I don't know what had gotten into me that day – perhaps it was hormones. As soon as he let me up off the concrete I started "chirping" at him again, only this time I was heading in the other direction towards my own house. He quickly followed in pursuit. The adrenaline was pumping throughout my body and my heart was racing in anticipation of a possible fight. I had never been in a fight. This would be my first – and last. We both raised our fists and stood toe-to-toe shuffling for the best position to land a punch. I threw the first punch, and to my astonishment it landed squarely on the bridge of Bill's nose. Blood immediately started pouring out of his nostrils and it was everywhere. It was the only punch thrown in the fight.

I wasn't very proud of myself after what happened and my friendship with Bill was never quite the same. I gained a new-found respect for what can happen when you respond aggressively towards someone who is already upset.

I learned from my mother that we do not have the right to behave in an unkind manner towards someone who does something inappropriate to us. It is important to treat others with kindness regardless of the way they are feeling, and always do unto others as we would have them do unto us.

If someone throws a stone at you, you throw back a piece of bread.

11

Every pot has a lid somewhere that fits.

When people heard that I was taking a journey to retrace my life, the first question they asked was, "Why do you want to go back?" I asked myself why I would want to set foot in a place where I was born, where I used to have dozens of relatives, knowing there would be no one waiting for me. Why would I want to revisit the hell of the concentration camps where my family had been murdered and I had been imprisoned?

I wanted to share this journey with others, to show them what hate has done in the past and is capable of doing in the future if we don't pay attention to the warning signs. I hope that the younger generations following us can learn from my experiences and do what is necessary to stop it from happening. That was an important reason why I had to make the journey. I knew it wouldn't be easy, but that was okay. I am a survivor who has dealt with more difficult things in my life. All my life I have dealt with problems by facing them, taking one step at a time. It took courage to go back into the darkness, but I found light there too.

Was the trip worth it? Absolutely. It was a journey I thought I would never take, but I am pleased that I chose to take it. I have more sadness now than I did before, and I know that after what I experienced on this journey, my life will never be the same. My mind is working overtime now, always searching for more information, more answers. It's an endless search; sometimes the more you search, the more you want to know. The journey has made me even more committed to making presentations about my life, especially to schools. I came away from the trip feeling that I am not doing enough, that I should be doing more. Seeing what I did on this trip has reinforced in me the *importance of showing people what hate can do. I hope my story will convince students of the importance of compassion, love, and respect for all mankind.*

My feelings, my life, and my message have all changed because of the trip. When I first got back, I couldn't deal with it. I couldn't even go outside and face people for the first few days. If someone asked me about the trip, I started to cry. All I could say was "devastating" and walk away. But the best thing I did was get back to work, even though at first I broke down when I opened my mouth. However, I don't feel bad for crying, because I'm not ashamed of my tears. People need to see that I can laugh and cry.

At some point you have to decide whether you are going to let your pain control you or you are going to control your pain. I have to live with the pain, but I want to control my own destiny. I look around and see people in pain trying to fix it with alcohol and medication. They are not dealing with the pain; they're too afraid to deal with it. We have to make choices as to how we're going to deal with the good and the bad that happens to us. We have to accept responsibility for our actions and not blame God or somebody else. The choices we made yesterday affect us today, and the choices we are making right now will affect us tomorrow.

When I was young my mother didn't want to tell me much about her past. I knew that she was a Holocaust survivor, but she didn't share any details with me until I was in university and I started asking her some questions about it for a paper I was writing.

When my oldest daughter, Brenna, was in Grade 8 her teacher told her, "You should interview your grandmother on the war." After the teacher read Brenna's assignment she called my mother and asked if she would come into the Grade 7 and 8 class and talk about the Holocaust. She agreed, and that was the end of 50 years of silence. I remember it happening, and not being particularly interested in how it would affect my mother. I now have a better understanding of the courage it must have taken for her to speak publicly about what she had been through in the camps. Since that first presentation in 1996 I've seen her speak a number of times, and witnessed the pain that she goes through each time. I don't how she does it day-in and day-out, sometimes three times a day. I ask myself, "Why does she put herself through this over and over again?" My mother says she does it to pass on important lessons to the next generation about tolerance, acceptance, compassion and behaving responsibly towards each other. When I watch her I feel like it's more about letting go of the pain that she has buried deep down inside. Whatever the reason, it must be having a positive affect because the public demand for her to speak keeps growing, and she continues to be strong and healthy.

Shortly after my mother spoke to Brenna's class other schools in the region starting requesting her presentation. I can't remember how it all got started, but over the course of the next couple of years it seemed like the phone was ringing on a daily basis, and without any formal marketing, the word of her talks had spread enough that she was quickly becoming more in demand. My mother had discovered a new mission. It was taking up more and more of her time and becoming the focus of everything she was doing.

I chose to keep my distance from everything that was happening to her. Everyone was so worried about my mother and how she would handle all of the driving to the various speaking engagements that were taking her farther and farther away from home. I started wondering whether I would eventually have to drive her around, but fortunately someone else always stepped in to help her when she really needed the help. Her best friend Jackie was a great help to her, but most of the time she drove herself. I was absorbed with my own problems. As a result, I didn't give my mother the support that she deserved.

When my mother decided to write her first book I was thrilled for her, but I wasn't particularly optimistic about the response she would receive once it was published. I tried to advise her regarding the realities of trying to sell a self-published manuscript, but she chose to ignore me and went ahead and printed 2000 copies. They were all gone in six months.

As my mother's life changed, I continued to feel strongly that it was important for me to keep my distance from what was going on. I thought that she had a mission based on her own experiences, and that I had my path, a different one, to follow. My mother was disappointed that I didn't read her book when it was first published. For some reason I didn't want to read it immediately. I now believe that I was too preoccupied with my own problems, worried about being smothered by her attention, and still trying to establish my own independence – even though I was forty-six years-of-age.

When my mother decided to go back to her hometown in Hungary and retrace her steps through the camps, I was the logical person to accompany her on her journey. I encouraged her to go and took responsibility for hooking her up with the film producer who would make the documentary film she created about the journey. Despite keeping my hand in her initiatives, I still maintained a comfortable distance from her. Although I don't regret my decision, I haven't figured out why I didn't want to make the trip.

In 2007, shortly after returning from my trip back to Europe, I went back into town to shop. People who knew of my trip would approach me with big hugs, and showing their emotions, they would ask me how my trip was. How could I describe 28 days of hell? I would respond by saying that I was devastated – and then I would break down. One day I returned to find Jan already home from work. He asked me, "How are you?" I explained to my son, "I have a difficult time facing people." Jan's response was, "Oh yes, I know all about life." I must say I was shocked by his response. The only way I could justify his comment was by saying to myself, "Oh my God! He must have had a horrible day at work."

I don't underestimate the emotional challenges my son experienced living with a mother who is a Holocaust survivor. How we deal with our challenges depends on the choices we make. My son's response was not what I had hoped to hear. We think we understand everything but that's not humanly possible.

It wasn't until I decided to write this book with my mother that I really took the time to know and understand her journey. I finally came to accept what she had been through – and fully appreciate the determination and resiliency that she has demonstrated throughout her life. I now realize it's not too late to learn from her experiences and apply the wisdom to my own life. I need to give back to my mother the love that she gave so generously to me and find the inner-passion and purpose of my own journey. What would happen if we all had the same courage to find our passion and purpose like my mother did? How would it change our lives? Surely, there is a lid that fits everyone's pot.

While working on this manuscript my mother made a comment about the possibility of retiring in the future. I looked at her and said, "Come on, mom, you know you will never retire. You'll keep speaking right up until the end – until you are no longer able to physically get in front of an audience." She agreed that retirement was unlikely.

I learned from my mother the importance of finding purpose in life. It takes courage to look beyond the disappointments and painful experiences from our past and not let them control our future. It's not too late to learn from our experiences and apply the wisdom to our lives – and in the process reach our destiny.

12

Only a stone should live alone.

It started for me on September 14, 2010 in the small town of Port Elgin. I was nearing the end of a speaking engagement and had the last slide of my PowerPoint presentation projected on the screen. It was my wedding portrait. My husband Rude had given me red and white carnations for my wedding bouquet. September has always been an emotional time for me as it reminds me of my 19-year marriage to Rude which ended with his death in September of 1964. I like to end my presentations with the slide of our wedding portrait and talk a little about the wonderful relationship I had with my husband. At the end of my presentation a teacher came up on stage and handed me a dozen red and white carnations – she had read in my book about the wedding bouquet and wanted to acknowledge my husband's passing. About a week later, on the actual anniversary of his death, I was in Sudbury and the students presented me with two dozen roses, one yellow and one white. The white roses commemorated my husband and the yellow roses commemorated my twin daughter, who passed away at the time of birth.

I have been alone for many years. I would say it has not been by choice but rather more by circumstance. My busy speaking schedule keeps me travelling and it has been difficult to find a new partner. It isn't a good feeling to be alone, but I have learned to live with the situation. Many years ago after my husband Rude passed away I met a man at a wedding. At the time I was single and we developed a very nice relationship. He presented himself to me as a great family man, which attracted me to him because I wanted to be with someone who had the same values as me. After a few years of courting we got married. At that point I didn't realize there were issues, such as alcohol abuse and a heavy caffeine and nicotine addiction. A friend of mine came over to visit one evening and noticed that my husband had several drinks over a short period of time. She asked me, "Does he always drink like that?" I wasn't aware of the drinking because during my 19 years of marriage with Rude we didn't have alcohol in our home, except maybe at Christmas. Gradually the drinking got worse. Instead of being an evening activity, the drinking started at noon, and when I approached my husband about seeking help he refused. I didn't want to go to bed with a bottle; I wanted to go to bed with a man. I remember saying to my husband one evening as we were sitting in the family room in front of the fireplace, "It would be nice to have a little glass of sherry or a small glass of brandy to be romantic." His response was, "Romance is for kids."

I suggested we go for couples counseling and we went several times over a number of years. The counselors told me that addictive personalities can also be very possessive, and that was the truth for my husband. Living with someone who had an addictive personality put me under a lot of stress. If I made my son chicken soup or cookies my husband resented it. As one therapist said to him, "Are you trying to tell a Jewish mother not to give her son chicken soup?" He also resented my grandchildren and I used to find notes all over the house that he had made to keep records of how much time I was spending with them and what television shows we were watching together. At that point I was starting to realize that I would live longer if I lived alone.

Late one Sunday afternoon, I arrived home from visiting my girl-friend. Shortly after my arrival I went to the kitchen to begin preparing dinner, while my husband was sitting downstairs watching sports. Eventually he came upstairs and began yelling at me for no apparent reason. To this day I don't know what he was saying or why he was so upset. I saw that he was frothing at the mouth so I knew he had been drinking. He came towards me and pushed me up against the kitchen stove. It really scared me. I was so frightened that I decided to proceed with a separation. When I told him I wanted the separation he responded by saying, "How are you going to pay the utility bills and drive your car?" I told him, "No matter what, I will not sell my soul for a meal ticket."

Most relationships begin as a result of one person being attracted to another. As young adults we not only fall in love with another person but also with the idea of love – the sensations of the physical attraction and the feelings of being connected because we now have a boyfriend or girlfriend. But quite often when we think we have fallen in love we are not focusing on deep friendship, which needs to develop first in order to create a lasting relationship.

Looking back I realize that the attributes I thought my husband had were just wishful thinking on my part. I was looking for a healthy, happy relationship and because of my desire, I accepted what I was told as being the truth – though I came to see it was a lie. I was very disappointed in myself. How did I allow myself to see something that wasn't even there? It took me some time to get over what had happened, but I welcomed being alone and the opportunity to regain my serenity and inner peace. I haven't remarried for 23 years. My mother used to say, "Only a stone should live alone." I can see that it is becoming more difficult to find a partner the older I get. But I have learned not to rush into a new relationship, and be certain about the reasons why I want to connect with another person. Time never runs out until you die and in the meantime I keep hoping that somewhere, somehow, someone is waiting for me. I am 86 years old and I am still looking.

What are we looking for in a partner? What are the real reasons we find ourselves attracted to someone? How can we make sure we choose the right partner who suits our soul?

When I made the decision to leave my marriage of 25 years, everything came to a head. It was an extremely challenging time in my life, but it was liberating for me because I finally made the decision to change my life, despite the impact I knew it would have on my family – and the impact on my mother was devastating. She told me that I was "pulling the rug out from under her." My decision was going to displace her from the home where she thought she would spend the rest of her days.

When my wife and I built our home I thought it might be a good idea to have my mother come and live with us. By bringing my mother onto our property we were ensuring that she would have the care she needed as she approached the twilight years of her life. Adding her residence to our existing home also helped us complete our dining room, build our porches and finish the landscaping. It seemed like a good decision at the time. I talked my mother into selling her waterfront home and my wife agreed to have her build a self-contained in-law suite that was attached to our house. The decision to build my mother's residence next to our home created a lot of stress between my wife and me. I needed to support my wife's wishes but knew we weren't being very inclusive with my mother. Inviting her over for dinner three times a year didn't demonstrate to her that she was welcome in our home. My mother was feeling like she was being locked out. When I found the courage to leave my marriage I felt very guilty about having asked my mother years earlier to sell her waterfront home and give up the independent lifestyle she had worked so hard for. Now the house she lived in was going to be sold and, at 86-years-of-age, she was going to have to find another place to live. The fact that I have displaced my mother leaves me saddened and embarrassed. I need to take full responsibility for my decisions.

It could have been the end of our relationship; however, out of my personal need to reconnect with my mother, I started to talk to her about the things I hadn't discussed for a long time. I shared the truth about some of the situations I had experienced throughout my adult life and it helped her to have a better understanding of my situation. The support that I had received from my mother as a young child was still there. I also began to realize and acknowledge to her that some of my decisions had resulted in her being treated unfairly. She had deserved more than I had given her as my mother. Slowly, we started to rebuild our relationship and now have a renewed interest and commitment to helping each other through life.

I am no different than any other mother; I want my son to be happy. When our children get married we hope they make the right choices and find a lifetime partner. We all want to see our children accomplish this and live a happy life. Unfortunately, that's not the reality of life. I knew my son was suffering for a long time. I agree with him when he describes me as having been devastated. However, it is very difficult to deal with any situation when you only know half the truth, which is all I had until the day Jan shared some information that I had no knowledge of. Sometimes we voice our opinions when we don't have all of the information. I have learned that this can be very dangerous. In the end the truth will prevail.

Only a stone should live alone.

I learned from my mother that good relationships are built upon a foundation of deep friendship. When we are comfortable being with ourselves we are able to take the time necessary to cultivate a lasting connection with another person based on truth.

13

Facts do not cease to exist
because they are ignored.

*I received an email from a young man by the name of Eli who had
been searching for his relatives on the Internet when he found me.
When he discovered that I was his grandmother's sister he thought
there must have been some kind of mistake. So Eli emailed his third
cousin, Haim, who filled him in on some of the historical background
regarding the relationship between his grandmother and myself. His
cousin made it sound like my sister and I had caused a separation
in the family as a result of a disagreement between her and me. Eli
explained to me that he was open-minded and he would like to know*

more about me. I had previously received a similar email from Haim after he had read my autobiography and just like Eli, he wrote to me that he had no knowledge about our family life in Europe when I was growing up. He also explained that he had no knowledge about what his mother Fradel and I had endured in the concentration camps during the Holocaust. I returned his email and included my phone number, welcoming him to call me. The following morning I received a phone call from Israel, but unfortunately, I was not home and missed the call.

I often wonder why my sister never spoke about what life was like in our family as we were growing up. Is it easier for her to live in denial? Fradel has ten children, 100 grandchildren, and many great and great-great grandchildren who were never told the true facts about our childhood, the family dynamics, our camp experiences, and her denial of my existence after the war. Most of the family does not know I exist.

Children reach a point in their maturation and development when they are ready to receive more information. Eli was shocked to find me on the Internet. I have learned how important it is to communicate *the truth to teenagers. It can be very painful for young adults to find out that their parents have been lying to them and they lose trust. When they are old enough to ask questions they should not be ignored and the truth should never be denied.*

I wasn't entirely aware of my family background when I was growing up. My father's heritage was Swedish and we celebrated some of his Scandinavian traditions in our home. I remember as a very young child travelling to the city with my parents to celebrate a traditional Swedish Christmas Eve. We sang traditional Swedish Christmas songs with many other families, while children danced around the wreath.

I am fortunate to have spent time with some of my relatives on my father's side of the family. One of my cousins came to visit us in 1960, and after my father's car accident his mother came over in 1962. After Grade 12 I travelled to Sweden on my own for three months to visit my relatives. I visited my two uncles and their families and travelled extensively throughout Sweden and Norway. It was also an opportunity to improve my ability to speak Swedish. My father wanted me to learn English first, then

Swedish, when I was growing up. One of the most memorable parts of my trip was enjoying all of the pickled herrings and flat-breads. It reminded me of sitting around the breakfast table with my mother and father trying all of those delicious foods. All of these experiences have contributed to the strong connection I feel to my Swedish heritage.

There wasn't a lot of discussion around the table about my Jewish background, though there were signs that something was different about my mother's heritage. She was an amazing cook. The Hungarian goulash, cabbage rolls, potato latkes, Jewish chicken soup and Eastern European desserts were unlike any other meals I experienced at my friends' homes. I remember my mother spending hours in the kitchen creating these fantastic meals, and allowing me to eat as much as I wanted. I loved exploring the deep recesses of her kitchen cupboards where there were cookies and cinnamon buns tucked away in little round tins. During my last year of high school I was involved in a project to beautify the front of our school with shrubs and a seating area for students. During the eight-day Passover holiday my mother made potato latkes and brought them over to the school for everyone who was working on the project.

I found another sign that my mother's background was different and very disturbing. There were the black and white photos, tucked away in a small box in the closet, that my dad had received in Sweden from a man who worked at the Polish Embassy. The pictures were in a camera that had been taken away from a Nazi guard at the end of the war. They were gruesome. The image of a young child in one photo, perhaps four or five years old, lying dead on top of a pile of emaciated adults, remains etched in my mind – but there was very little discussion about what it all meant. My mother was not talking about the Holocaust at that time in her life.

I have come to appreciate why my mother makes the effort to keep the lines of communication open in our family. She always shows a willingness to make herself available to discuss issues and concerns of importance, and though it can be difficult at times to have these conversations, they have helped us maintain a close relationship to this day. While helping to raise my three children she also kept the lines of communication open with them. They would spend many hours with her in the garden and around the kitchen stove which created wonderful opportunities for them to ask her questions.

I have often confided in my mother about the difficult situations I was experiencing in my life, trusting that she would keep the details of my personal issues between the two us. It's the way it has always been for as long as I can remember. However, as the years went by, we found our conversations becoming increasingly more frustrating for both of us. We recently discussed this trend and agreed that this was a new pattern.

After I graduated from high school, my mother purchased a waterfront building lot in the Huntsville, Ontario area, where we decided to build a cottage. It was a very exciting time in our family as we pursued a goal that was once my father's dream. He loved spending time in the wilderness and took my mother and me to fish on weekends and holidays. My mother had never experienced fishing in Europe but was willing to learn so she could spend time with my father. She grew to love fishing, and she loved to cook the fish for the family to eat. The tradition of fishing carried on at the lake in Huntsville where we were building each weekend. There was always a group of friends travelling north to help me build the cottage and we had a great time together working, skiing and fishing. My mother always caught her share of the fish. I remember her picture being in the local newspaper for catching a three-pound-four-ounce Speckled Trout on the end of an alder branch. The fish fry was a highlight of the day. After a great meal my mother would let us taste a small glass of Hungarian Pear Brandy and we would share fishing stories and laugh. My mother and I had finally reached a point where we had learned to deal with the pain of my father's passing. We were at peace and grateful for the things we had to share with each other.

When my mother and I reflect upon those amazing years at the lake we realize that our relationship became strained after I got married and she started providing childcare for my kids. I am blessed to have three great children, but the strain of my relationship with my wife and our differing views on parenting took its toll on my relationship with my mother. During the thousands of hours my mother provided childcare she had disagreed with many of the decisions my wife and I made. I felt like I was stuck in the middle. I know my mother wanted me to do everything I could to make the relationship with my wife work, which is why she chose never to interfere with our parenting decisions. However, she was becoming concerned about the amount of anger I was feeling inside. I realize now that I was consumed with my own issues and took advantage of my mother's generosity and the support she had provided for my family over many years.

I was aware of the huge frustrations Jan was experiencing through some of his difficult times. It's not easy when you find yourself between a rock and a hard place. From time-to-time I felt I made a big mistake agreeing to give up the privacy I had in my own home. The only good thing that came out of it was that while the children were still home I was able to provide a haven for them, or they could call me and say, "Bubba, would you pick me up from school?" or "Would you pick me up at the bus stop?" The idea was for me to become part of the family. Nothing could be further from the truth. I only became a happy caring Bubba.

Facts do not cease to exist because they are ignored.

As a high-school principal, I thought a lot about the teenagers who came to school with poor attitudes, low motivation, and limited expectations for personal success. Many of them arrived each day with issues that affected their self-esteem, emotions, and their ability to focus on what we were trying to teach them. I wondered what kinds of conversations they were having at home. Could they ask questions and speak openly? Were there unanswered questions about what was going on in their homes and between their parents?

There is a question of personal vulnerability involved in speaking the truth. Everyone has a slightly different interpretation of the facts and has emotional insecurities that make it difficult at times to accept the viewpoint of others. Religious beliefs are a good example of this, and are what ultimately caused my mother's sister to deny my mother's existence. Adults can influence a teenager's perception by striving to build a positive relationship based on openness and trust, and not ignoring the truth. It also requires a willingness to engage in the types of courageous conversations where individuals take responsibility for sharing how they feel about a situation in an honest, caring, compassionate and respectful way. One of the most powerful ways to improve communication, whether it's with a teenager, between friends or among adults, is to tell the truth about ourselves. The world is not a battleground where the goal is always to come out of a conversation being right. Simply admitting our own mistakes or asking for help when we don't know how to do something can build trust. If we take responsibility for our mistakes then we are better able to share our experiences with our children, speaking the truth about the situation and what we have learned from our successes and failures.

It has taken me a long time to learn these lessons from my mother. Unfortunately, my children did not experience an environment where it was easy to sit down and have an open conversation about the issues that were bothering them. Sometimes it happened one-on-one; however conversations involving the whole family were much more difficult to orchestrate. This often led to inconsistencies and misunderstandings around the feelings and expectations my wife and I had about raising the children. I know these inconsistencies affected my children in a negative way.

I learned from my mother that children need to know the truth when they are ready to receive more information. When parents are willing to keep the lines of communication open with their children, they provide an opportunity to discuss issues and concerns of importance.

We must not underestimate
our children's ability to understand.

I was fourteen when we rented a bungalow a block away from our two-room apartment. This place had been owned by Mr. Lefcovich, an elderly gentleman who used to sit outside in the summer watching us go to the square to get water. Soon after, my parents sent me to stay overnight with an old lady we called Zali Neni, who lived a block away. They told me she was very sick, but actually she was dying. I guess they didn't want to tell me the truth because I was so young. It is a Jewish belief that a person should not die alone, so I slept there every night for a week and in the morning an older woman arrived to stay with her during the day. However, I was a sheltered fourteen-year-old, and the sounds of her dying are still with me today. One morning the older woman left a few minutes after she arrived; I didn't know why. An hour later she returned with ten men, a minion, *required by Jewish rites to say the prayers for the dead*. Then I knew Zali had died during the night. I have always believed that there is a lot more to be gained by including rather than excluding. It would have been better to tell me the truth about the fact that I was sleeping with a dying woman. I was never given the opportunity to get involved, even to feel for her or be compassionate for her because my parents did not believe I was capable of understanding. Parents need to have faith in their children and give them the opportunity to be involved.

In October of 2010 I was on a speaking tour in Alberta, and did ten presentations to secondary, junior high and elementary schools. When I arrived I was informed that Grade 3 students would also be included in all elementary school assemblies. Over my 14-year speaking experience I had never presented to students that young before, because I wasn't sure about how much they would be able to understand. I was also concerned that the parents would not like their children to *be part of the assembly and hear what happened during the Holocaust. I agreed to do the presentations and parents were given the opportunity to leave their kids at home or come and be part of the audience. I modified my presentation by removing some of the more graphic pictures that I would normally show to teenagers and didn't talk about what happened in the gas chambers. I was blown away by the childrens' ability to understand what a bad thing it is to be a bully or a bystander, as well as the detailed questions that resulted. When I described the making of the dirty potato-peel soup one Grade 3 student commented, "I guess you got the potato peels and the Nazis got the potato." Some of the parents that attended came over to me after my presentation and thanked me on behalf the children. The experience gave the parents an opportunity to appreciate their children's ability to understand. As one principal pointed out, it's okay for children to be sad and feel the pain of others. However, the important thing is to explain to the children that what happened is real and is not a Hollywood movie.*

My mother taught me that even though a situation in life does not have a happy ending, there is something to be learned from every story – and this is an important way that we can guide children. As an educator, every day presented opportunities for learning.

The weight room at the local high school where I taught physical education for ten years consisted of one multi-station apparatus and a freestyle bench. The equipment was tucked away in a small classroom on another floor, far away from the gymnasium. Based on my department's concern for student safety and the lack of teacher supervision, I convinced my principal to move the weight room to a classroom one floor up and across from the gym. Department funding was used to purchase additional equipment so that a small group of students in each physical education class could go across the hall and exercise.

I created a weightlifting club by charging students a nominal fee for use of the room at lunch, and before and after school. These funds were used to buy more equipment and do the necessary maintenance and repairs. Membership grew quickly to over 50 students and athletic teams were encouraged to sign out the room for training purposes. Staff also took advantage of the opportunity to work out during lunch and after school alongside the kids. Interest in the new facility was so positive that the department developed two new courses based on student survey responses, one for males, and one for females, with a focus on personalized training. Increased student enrollment in these courses helped bring more budget money to the department and the facility continued to get better equipment over time.

Having adequate space became the new challenge. Once again, I convinced my principal to allow for an expansion of the weight room into the adjoining classroom, which required knocking out the wall between the two rooms. Our weight training club had grown to 100 students. Senior students were chosen to act as leaders and mentors. Their responsibilities included supervising junior students, cleaning, reporting equipment problems, and doing minor equipment repairs. The department timetabled seven classes into the two rooms over two semesters. Local community user groups that wanted access to the facility in the evenings had to sign a contract and make a financial donation to the program.

The physical improvements made to the weight room over a

three-to four-year period had a number of positive outcomes for our school. Students used the room responsibly and respectfully, and there were no incidents of theft, vandalism or graffiti over that period of time. Not one of the students had their weight room privileges removed or required disciplining for inappropriate behaviour. There was a significant increase in the number of staff and students participating together in physical fitness and students attended class regularly and on time.

There is the potential to underestimate the ability of young people to act responsibly. What the weight room experience taught me was the importance of getting students involved in the decision-making process from the beginning, and then giving them the opportunity to take control of their future. By the time I became a vice-principal I had forgotten this important lesson. I had to quickly relearn what I now know to be true about working with kids. Sometimes a student's learning is more meaningful when they are asked to take responsibility for a negative situation by providing solutions.

The school where I was appointed vice-principal had a serious graffiti problem. Students were heavily tagging the building inside and out using spray paint and magic markers. The maintenance staff attempted to remove the graffiti using very expensive paint sealer, with marginal success. With the assistance of a technology design teacher, digital photos of markings in the washrooms were taken, copied and distributed to staff along with a memo requesting an unobtrusive notebook check of every student in the school.

I received a call from a teacher with a message about a student wanting to leave the classroom with a red and black magic marker. The teacher thought this was unusual and might be of interest to my investigation. I went to the classroom and brought the student down to my office, where I conducted a search that revealed tags in the student's notebook matching the digital photos taken in the washrooms.

The student received four consequences: a suspension, a police charge of mischief, painting all the washrooms throughout the school, and a tour of 23 intermediate classrooms with the community police officer and myself to apologize and discuss with the students the impact of his behaviour on the school. I was trying to follow the idea of using a punishment along with restitution and reconciliation on the part of the guilty student. I now realize that these four consequences were heavy on punishment and light on responsibility.

Following this incident, I approached the grade ten visual arts teachers about involving their students in beautifying the washrooms throughout the school. It seemed like an excellent way to get the students involved on a personal level and a positive way for them to change their physical environment. Designs were submitted and funds were raised to support the students' work. The project was a huge success. The washrooms ended up having some very interesting student art work in them, and the graffiti problem disappeared – never to return.

When I finally became principal I decided to resolve a situation that had been a serious problem for many years at the same school. The school has five sets of doors providing students with access to the outside of the building. Two of them led out to a ramp that borders the town side of the school, one set at the top of the ramp and one at the bottom. Students who are walking to and from downtown, before and after school, and during the lunch period, use the doors at the top of the ramp.

The ramp had been a hangout for about 50 to 60 of the toughest kids we had at the school. Students went there to socialize, have a cigarette, hide while skipping classes, gather for a fight, or engage in other inappropriate activities such as drug dealing. The ramp environment was a challenging situation to manage because the group at the top of ramp did not get along with the group at the bottom. Sometimes the two groups would drift into each others' territory and a fight would break out. There could be 100 students standing in a circle watching while two students were fighting. Often they weren't our students. Because the ramp was so close to town, former students, students from other schools, dropouts and drifters would come to the area looking to sell drugs, connect with friends or resolve a conflict with someone.

I wanted to try a student-centered approach to solving the ramp problem, and avoid using punishment. I started by going out to the ramp to talk with them about the problem. I wanted the students to understand that the behaviours that typically took place on the ramp were unacceptable to the school and the community. I called for a meeting in the main office between administration, our community police officer, and the students who were using the ramp. During the meeting, I explained the concerns brought forward by the staff, parents and other members of the community. I tried to discuss the options we had to change the ramp situation, but was met with a lot of resistance. One student said I would never be successful in moving students off the ramp because "her father and her father's father grew up fighting on the ramp." Things got a little emotional at times, but I let them finish talking as long as they weren't rude or disrespectful. There were three more meetings with the students over the next couple of weeks to continue the discussion and brainstorm solutions. Each time we met they seemed a little more receptive to the idea of making the ramp an out-of-bounds area and moving themselves to another place. The turning point came when we agreed to create a new space where benches would be provided and the students could paint the area with artwork. It was also good for the school because the new area was more visible and allowed administration to better supervise the students. It was a wonderful warm spring day when we undertook the project of cleaning up the new area for kids to hang out and socialize. There was a lot of winter dirt and garbage, and the students did a great job of cleaning it up. A boundary area was marked off with spray paint, and heavy-duty picnic tables and garbage cans were moved into position and given a fresh coat of paint. From then on the students did not hang out on the ramp, as it was not the cool place to be.

It took me seven years to find the courage to have the conversations needed with the students to solve the ramp problem. During that time I had focused on suspension instead of involving the students in the solution – and this time they came through with flying colours. At home, school, or in the workplace, teenagers need to be given the opportunity to contribute to their own lives; after all, they will be fully responsible for themselves in a very short time – so why not have them practice now?

I learned from my mother that children respond best when

they are given responsibility and treated with respect. Shielding children from reality will not help them develop a deeper understanding about situations that exist in life. Parents have a responsibility to explain to their child what is happening, so that they are able to better understand.

We must not underestimate our children's ability to understand.

15

A mother's children are a portrait of herself.

After one of my evening presentations a senior adult came to the microphone and commented, "I noticed that you became emotional when you talked about your father." He wanted to know why I was not as emotional when I spoke about other members of my family. The first thing that came to my mind was that I wasn't sure why I became emotional speaking about my father. I explained to the audience that my father and I had challenges based on religious differences and we didn't have the opportunity to work things out before the Holocaust. Perhaps after so many years I wish that opportunity had been available for me.

We bond with our parents – some of us with our father and some of us with our mother – and the reason I bonded with my mom was because she gave me life. At the time when my mother found out that she was pregnant with me she was unwell. The doctor told her that she must have an abortion. In the high orthodox beliefs abortion is out of the question and if a mother is ill they try to save the child before they would abort the child and try to save the mother. My mother decided to stay in bed for the whole pregnancy in an attempt to bring another life into this world. As I get older I realize how difficult it must have been for her lying in bed for eight months when she already had three children and was living in a one-room house with no hydro or indoor plumbing. I had a grade three student ask me, "Was your mother your angel?" and I said, "Yes, more than once."

The most important thing I learned from my mom was to be compassionate – as she was. Despite our poverty, she always shared with others who had less than we did, sometimes food or a pot to cook in. She had a big aluminum pot where the linens were boiled on the wood stove and that pot used to travel up and down the street for *those that wanted to use it for the same purpose. These days, children will often be sent to get take-out food if the mother is not well. The fact that my mother always made our clothes and cooked for us, even when she was sick, was an unselfish act of love. Students often ask me what was the most painful time for me during the Holocaust. The pain now is the same as it was 65 years ago – the way my mom vanished in seconds and I never had the chance to say "goodbye" to her or say "I'm sorry if I disobeyed you."*

Some of us reflect on the way our mothers were with us when we were little and we try to do the same things with our own children. When times were difficult in my own life I made sure that I was there and caring for my son just like my mother was for me. It was important for me to be there for him because I became a widow and we both were in a lot of pain. At that particular point in time, my focus was on listening to my son and making sure that I was always available for him to speak to me when he was upset. When Jan was hurt, I was thankful that he could come to me and I was available to give him some advice. As a 19-year-old, my son appreciated the value of the truth, which he learned from our discussions. I knew I needed to go to work for financial reasons, but I chose to stay home until he went to high school in order to provide a secure and safe home for him so that he could deal with his emotional pain. No amount of money can buy what our children need – time spent with a mother.

My friends and colleagues often ask me, "What is it like to be the son of a Holocaust survivor?" My response is, "My mother is a hard act to follow. She doesn't let me off the hook with anything I do." At times I have criticized her directly to her face. I recognize that it will not reflect very well on me if I publicly criticize her when sharing with others how incredibly difficult is has been to maintain a positive relationship with her. My friends interpret my response as meaning that my mother is a great role model and that she has high expectations of me – and I am finally realizing that this has been my issue all along. My mother has never given me a bad word of advice. The problem was I didn't want to hear it. I am listening a lot more carefully these days.

While working on this manuscript I found the courage to be honest with my mother and share with her the pressure I was feeling being her son. I told her that I felt like I was constantly sitting on the edge of my chair. My personal difficulties, no matter how serious, could never compete with her horrific experiences in the concentration camps of the Holocaust. Sometimes trying to relate to my mother feels like being in a Monty Python movie; you lose an arm, then a leg, and then finally someone chops off your head, but you try to keep going like nothing has happened because it's still a hell of a lot better than having to go through the Holocaust.

When Jan talks about having a hard time being my son and how he felt that I didn't let him off the hook for anything he did, he covers a lot of territory. I have let him off the hook with a lot of things and there were also things that he chose to do whether I agreed with him or not. It seems to me like he sees me as a very controlling mother that had complete control of his life. Personally, I feel that some of this is perception on Jan's part.

I know I did what any good mother would do by always trying to support my son, particularly when it came to his health issues. A person's health is the number one concern because without it there isn't much left. At one point I travelled to Toronto with Jan and his daughter Brenna to help babysit while he went for medical treatment. I remember pushing her stroller along the streets of Toronto while Jan received colonic treatments on the Danforth. I went to the city with the two of them several times.

When it came to other issues such as Jan's frustrations in his career or his desire to move to the west coast, at times I couldn't give him what he wanted. I couldn't tell him what he wanted to hear, and realize that it must have been very frustrating for him as a young adult. I am pleased to see that as Jan gets older and matures he has a much more realistic viewpoint about what happened to him, and between us, over the years.

My mother tells the students in her audiences how important it is to deal with their challenges by having the courage to share with their parents the issues that are troubling them, when they can, before it's too late. My mother raised me to be open and speak up when I was upset or something didn't feel right. I was fortunate that she made the time to listen and never said "I haven't got the time now, we'll talk later." Despite the fact that at times I didn't feel that my mother understood me, or agreed with my decisions, she continued to support me every step of the way. She never abandoned me.

My mother is extremely intense. Sometimes I wish she would just lighten up and have a little more fun. Then again it's hard to have fun when there isn't anyone to have fun with. My family didn't do a very good job of including her in the things we did and I have to take responsibility for not including her more in our family celebrations. I was feeling trapped and failed to face my responsibility to tell my family that my mother must be included.

At 86 years-of-age my mother continues to enjoy excellent health, so I feel like I have been given the gift of time to reconnect with her. If I can help her achieve her goals then I am fortunate to have an opportunity to support her with the anticipation that there are still many good years ahead! I also recognize that it is no small coincidence that my mother and I are on very similar paths, which include sharing our life-experiences and helping others to understand theirs.

I learned from my mother how important our parental legacy is. How our children will care for their children will depend on the degree of love and compassion that we give and demonstrate to them.

A mother's children are a portrait of herself.

Afterword

A Legacy of Lessons

In this book I have stated the obvious – the ability of my mother to overcome challenging obstacles in her life, particularly the time spent in the death camps of the Holocaust, will not be understood by most individuals. But her story goes well beyond the recorded horrors of history – and it's what makes this woman so special.

My mother's father wrote 18 books, all on the topic of religion. She would wake up at two-o'clock in the morning and watch her father writing beside the petroleum lamp. Each day he would rise at 5:30 a.m. and head for the synagogue for morning prayers. During the day he taught religious studies, until one day he gave up teaching and started travelling on the road selling his books – just like my mother has been doing for 14 years. My mother didn't agree with her father's religious teachings; however, she did inherit his passion for learning, and his determination to make a difference in the lives of those he met along the way.

In the summer of 1968, for the first time in her life, my mother read a book. It was Victor Frankel's *Man's Search for Meaning*. She had to read it over and over until she was able to understand all the words and messages contained within it. My mother was 44 years-of-age. She authored her first book, now a national bestseller four-times-over, 32 years later. Nipissing University, in North Bay Ontario, granted her an Honorary Doctorate in 2005 for her extensive work promoting education in schools. The Royal College of Physicians and Surgeons of Canada made her an Honorary Fellow in 2008 for her work across Canada teaching compassion – an important element of the healing process. And in that same year, the Province of Ontario honoured her with the Order of Ontario for her contributions to the betterment of society – all amazing and unlikely accomplishments for an individual who, prior to reaching the age of 44, had never read a book!

From one generation to another, life-lessons are passed down that define each family's legacy. The lessons found within the pages of this book are my mother's. They form the framework that defines her efforts to – despite all of her challenges – raise a good son, as an individual with strong moral purpose, and the ability to apply that purpose to daily living. At the core of the framework are her values: compassion, love, trust, patience and acceptance. But most of all, her story and its message is about determination and perseverance – and how with these attributes, anything is possible over time. I believe her message to be true. She also challenges parents and their children to be courageous – in the same way that she was with me. Engaging in open communication about their feelings, families can examine the truth and decipher perception from reality, and in doing so, better prepare themselves to take responsibility for their choices – and the resulting consequences.

My family roots are linked to my grandfather and a century of writing and teaching. The overarching message in this book, passed down to me from my mother, is that there are no limits to what we can learn and accomplish when we take the time to examine who we are and our actions towards others. By acting compassionately, with love, and with perseverance and determination, we can achieve what we most desire and become who we are meant to be.

There are limits to what we can learn exclusively from formal education. I have seen this in my 30 years of teaching. Therefore, whether we are parents or teachers, we must commit to raising the whole child, not just the mind, but the body and the spirit. And when we do, our children will reach their greatest potential as citizens of the world.

I have been blessed to have the opportunity to work in education, including a 40-year connection with sport. Coaching youth provides a wonderful opportunity to teach commitment, determination, tolerance and kindness, among other attributes. I am thankful for these years. And I have learned a lot about myself trying to become the best role model I could be. When I was selected as one of Canada's Outstanding Principals I realized that I was on the right track with my efforts, and now my responsibility to pass on the values I have learned through my mother's legacy is even greater.

My mother and I look forward to meeting you during our travels on the road, sharing stories of hope and determination, and working together to build stronger legacies for our future generations.

About The Authors

Jan Olsson

Jan Olsson has been an elementary and secondary teacher, a high-school department head in physical and health education and student services, and a secondary vice-principal and principal. Jan is co-founder of Schools That Shine with Character, a national character education conference organized by Huntsville High School and the Trillium Lakelands District School Board in Ontario, Canada. In 2010 he was selected as one of Canada's Outstanding Principals by The Learning Partnership.

Jan completed his Masters of Character Education at the University of San Diego in 2008. He has spoken internationally on topics related to character education and leadership. His work has included presentations at The University of San Diego, Penn State University, the University Council for Education Administration in New Orleans, and to various school districts.

Jan's specific interests include moral development and ethics in administration, modelling affective communication and group decision-making to enhance organizational climate, and creating safe and inviting physical environments for learning.

Keep it Simple, Make it Real: Character Development in Grades 6-12 is his first book, which was released through Corwin Press in California in June 2009.

His second book, *Every Step of the Way*, was published in the spring of 2011. For information regarding keynote and workshop bookings visit www.thesimpleshift.com.

Jan may be contacted directly at thesimpleshift@gmail.com or by phone at 1-705-644-4063.

Eva Olsson

The outbreak of World War II plunged Eva into the heart of the Holocaust: concentration camps, slave labour factories, disease, and the deaths of millions, included most of her family.

Eva's strong faith in God and in herself has enabled her to maintain a positive focus throughout the rest of her life. For 50 years she remained silent about her experiences during the Holocaust, partly out of denial and partly out of fear it might happen again.

Since 1996 Eva has been speaking about her life in over 2000 schools, churches, meeting halls, conferences, colleges and universities, and to over one-and-a-half million individuals throughout Canada, in the hope that people who hear her story will know that it is possible to survive the worst that life has to throw at them. The response has been overwhelming. Thousands of letters from students have confirmed her hope that telling her story could make a difference in their lives. In 2007 Eva was invited to speak at the Institute of Peace and Justice at the University of San Diego.

The Ontario Secondary School Teachers Federation, community organizations, and schools have honoured Eva for her work on behalf of a more peaceful and tolerant world. Eva received an Honorary Doctorate from Nipissing University, North Bay Ontario in June 2005 and is a recipient of the Order of Ontario.

In September 2008, Eva was made an Honorary Fellow of the Royal College of Physicians and Surgeons of Canada.

An author and widely acclaimed public speaker, Eva makes presentations throughout Canada and the United States at public schools, colleges and universities, about tolerance, compassion and the consequences of hate and bullying. Her national bestselling book titled, *Unlocking the Doors: A Woman's Struggle Against Intolerance*, was released in 2001. Her second book, *Remembering Forever: A Journey of Darkness and Light* and a documentary film, *Stronger Than Fire: The Eva Olsson Story*, were released in the fall of 2008.

For information regarding keynote and workshop bookings visit www.evaolsson.ca. Eva may be contacted directly at eolsson@vianet.ca and by phone at 1-705-645-6055 or 1-888-477-2224.

About The Authors

Other Products by Jan Olsson

Keep It Simple, Make It Real:
Character Development in Grades 6-12

A powerful tool for influencing students'
attitudes and behaviours!

This resource provides school leaders with a comprehensive yet
practical framework for creating and sustaining a school-wide
character development program. Real-world scenarios tackle
tough issues such as vandalism, truancy, chronic tardiness, and
bullying, and demonstrate how to bring about positive change.

The book helps educators:

• Evaluate student behaviour, staff morale, and school climate

• Target real problems with commonsense strategies that can
  dramatically turn around student behaviour

• Assess a character development program's effectiveness

For product descriptions visit www.thesimpleshift.com

Other Products by Eva Olsson

Unlocking the Doors: A Woman's Struggle Against Intolerance

Remembering Forever: A Journey of Darkness and Light

Stronger Than Fire: The Eva Olsson Story
(Digital Video Disk)

Stronger Than Fire
(Audio Compact Disk)

For product descriptions visit www.evaolsson.ca

Presentations

A Legacy of Caring, Compassion and Character

Discover the role that family legacies
and positive relationships have in
shaping a child's identity and character.

**In this presentation Eva and Jan will discuss the importance
of establishing a positive and trusting relationship with children,
including how:**

- Family legacies mold our children's beliefs and patterns of behaviour
- A child forms a positive self-identity through the evolution
  of relationships
- A constructive family system can nurture a child's positive development
- Parents and educators can work together to support the success
  of each child on an individual basis

**For more information regarding presentations
visit www.thesimpleshift.com**